The Long Timetable

The Author with her Parents

The Long Timetable

Mary Oakeley

The Pentland Press Limited
Edinburgh • Cambridge • Durham • USA

First published in 1997 by
The Pentland Press Ltd.
1 Hutton Close
South Church
Bishop Auckland
Durham

British Library Cataloguing in Publication Data.
A catalogue record for this book is available
from the British Library.

ISBN 1 85821 510 2

Typeset by CBS, Felixstowe, Suffolk
Printed and bound by Bookcraft Ltd, Bath

To Rosemary and Rowland with
fondest love

ACKNOWLEDGEMENTS

To Mary Marshall for all her help

CONTENTS

ILLUSTRATIONS

CHILDHOOD

Chapter 1

Early Days

It was appropriate that I was born in a Girls' School! My Mother had gone to Bristol to be under the care of Dr Swayne, a famous gynaecologist, and as the family were moving from Wiltshire to Oxfordshire, she stayed in Clifton, Bristol for a month. Dr Swayne's nursing home was full, but as it was the school holidays he took over St Helen's, the school next door, and there I was born on 2 April 1913.

My brothers were not pleased about my arrival and suggested I should be thrown to the lions in the Bristol Zoo!

When I was a month old I was christened Mary, at a local church and then taken to The Gables, Eynsham, a beautiful old Tudor house which my Father had just bought. Up to this time Mother, Father, Atholl, Rosemary and Rowland had lived in a rented house in Rodbourne, Wiltshire but the lease had been terminated because the owners did not approve of my Father being a Liberal! My parents thought being near Oxford would be good for our education and nearer to London. My Father was keen on hunting and there were adequate stables for his hunters, and kennels for his Dandie Dinmonts.

The Gables was a beautiful old house, probably built about 1572. It had a large garden and an adjoining field. On the western side was a charming cottage, and an old malthouse, and since my Father did not care for noisy children, we lived in the cottage with our nurses. In actual fact, being a retired soldier from the South Lancashire Regiment he was called up in the First World War, and my mother lived by herself in The Gables with three maids, and two gardeners coming daily. At first there were two hunters but they became too expensive to keep after the war.

The years of childhood at The Gables were very happy ones. We saw little of our parents, though Mother could be summoned by a bell wired to her bedroom, if things went wrong, and sometimes they did! On one of Mother's visits she discovered the Nurse beating me unmercifully because I would not stop crying, and she was hastily despatched. I then had Nurse Hitch who was loved by me and hated by the others. On another

3

occasion the ceiling fell down in the night nursery, between my bed and Rosemary's, and it was a miracle neither of us was hurt.

Most people have fleeting memories of the years before hey were five. I remember the rocking horse where we spent many happy hours riding backwards and forwards, and also used the hole where the whip usually lived to pour down unpleasant food when Nurse was out of the room; the happy wet afternoons playing shipwreck or arranging our toys until Nurse came and made us put it all away as it was bedtime; and the joys of haymaking in the field where we made nests, of hay, and ended by riding in triumph on the top of the haywain as it went back to the farm.

One incident stands out in these years. My Father was at home for once and had been out on his horse, Mike. As he came up the drive, he called out we could ride back to the stables with him. My brother, Rowland and I had been playing soldiers, carrying large sticks, and I ran out carrying mine to be lifted up. As I ran I tripped over, and the stick went right through my face. I remember my Mother coming much upset, and taking me back to the house to be comforted, and soothed with Pomade de Vine, the remedy in those days for all cuts and bruises. Nevertheless I was to carry the scar for the rest of my life.

My Mother was delicate, and spent most afternoons resting on her sofa. We were always being told not to upset her or tire her. My Father had fought in the Boer War about which he had endless stories, which became all too well known to us in later years. There were, of course, certain disadvantages in being a soldier's daughter. When other children howled their heads off after a slight bump, we were brought up that 'soldiers' daughters don't cry', which could be very frustrating.

At one juncture my Mother went into a nursing home for a period and Aunt Josephine, an unmarried friend of the family came to supervise us. I think she must have found the whole episode most trying, as Nurse complained we had baked apples and rice pudding every day, and I wept solidly until Nurse suggested I was given a new book which diverted my attention. I learnt to read from a very early age and by the time I was three could read most of *Peter Rabbit*, though I still loved my Mother reading Bible stories to me.

When I was five significant changes took place in my life. Nurse Hitch departed amid a flood of tears and went off to nurse babies in Australia from where she sent many interesting books about the Gum Babies, and interested me in the Antipodes. I could just remember the end of the First World War, mainly because all the Union Jacks had been sold, and I had only a tattered Chinese one with which to celebrate. Doris came as a

The Author with May Brunyate

nursemaid in 1918 and I started school at Miss Swan's kindergarten.

Miss Swan was an excellent teacher and a firm disciplinarian. We learnt C-A-T Cat, B-A-T Bat and enjoyed *Reading without Tears.* For writing we did 'Pot hooks and hangers' and learnt to join them up. We learnt history from *Little Arthur's History of England;* geography from an ancient globe; and arithmetic from reciting our tables. Miss Swan played the piano and we learnt hymns and sang 'Loopy Loo'. At break we played in the garden singing 'Buttercups and Daisies in the Meadow', and enjoyed the 'Farmer's in his Den'.

On the mantelpiece of our one schoolroom were 'Objects of Warning'. One was a hard ball made up from wool collected by a little girl who chewed her blankets, and the wool which collected in her stomach made this hard ball, which had to be extracted in hospital. Another group of small objects had been found inside a cow which had died suddenly from unacceptable food provided by small children. All these horrors rested among a collection of Goss china from all over England and were used to teach us geography.

It was at Miss Swan's school that I received my first punishment. There were at this time eleven girls and one boy, Timmie, in the school. Because old Mrs Swan was bedridden and lay upstairs, we were not allowed to play noisy games, but one morning we decided to play Blind Man's Buff. Of course, Timmie was the blind man and we certainly made a lot of noise and Miss Swan came in. As I was the instigator of the game we were both punished with the school's worst punishment, which was to stand on a form in front of all the others at Morning Prayers. So there we stood, one each end with the tears streaming down our five-year-old faces, and our sobs accompanying the hymns.

The only other person I remember receiving this punishment was Phyllis who was caught with a roll of lavatory paper in her knickers. She was planning to take it home to trace some maps because we were supposed to draw them free-hand for our homework. She was very upset to be accused of stealing!

By the time I was seven life in the cottage had come to an end. Atholl was grown up and had gone to Sandhurst, and Rosemary and Rowland were away at boarding school. It became too difficult to keep it going for one child, but for a time I was put to bed in Mother's bed, and carried over to the cottage when Doris came back from her day out. Eventually I was moved over and slept in the little room off my Mother's bedroom.

I was often told how Father had beaten the older children with his riding crop and it hung above the dining-room mantelpiece for all to see. I lived in terror that I should receive this same punishment and I nearly did! Doris had taken me to a dancing class in the village and I was in a rage because I had to come back early. On the way home we were joined by Doris' young man and instead of holding my hand and talking to me, Doris clung to her lover and ignored me. I therefore ran off home in the dark by myself to teach her a lesson, but though Father was very angry I escaped a beating.

When I was seven, nearly eight, I caught paratyphoid. No one knew how I got it, though the general idea was it was either eating cream buns after the cinema where Father sometimes took us as a great treat, or from the filter which we used to purify our water. In those days there was no question of going to hospital, and the local doctor, Dr Cruickshank looked after me with the assistance of a Welsh nurse, Nurse Jones from the Acland hospital. For seven weeks I lay desperately ill in an age when there were no antibiotics. My Mother put me in her bed and slept on the sofa every night. I remembered her love and affection when years later she lay dying and I slept on the same sofa.

Each night during this long illness my Father came at five o'clock, and read the *Arabian Nights* to me. I still remember the adventures of Sinbad, and see my Father reading by lamplight each night. The others were sent to lodgings in the village while I was ill as they were in quarantine.

Eventually I recovered, and had to learn to walk again. As a great treat I was allowed to go out in the parish bath chair, a wicker affair which was kept at the vicarage. I was thrilled to be pushed down the village and to be greeted by many who thought I should never recover. To celebrate my recovery, my Father gave me a Dandie Dinmont puppy called Jilly whom I loved very dearly.

My Father loved his Dandie Dinmonts who were kept in the stables when the hunters went. They were extremely fierce and were always fighting. Every morning before breakfast, Father took them round the grounds and each day after lunch they went on a longer walk round some of the footpaths. Usually one of us had to go with him, and I remember how I hated going past a house where Moby Dog lived. The Dandies were on three double chains, and as we went along the narrow lane, Moby Dog would rush out and there would be a terrible fight with my Father yelling at me to get the dogs away; Mrs Moby cursing us all, and blood and hair flying in all directions.

The worst fight took place early one morning. This was among the Dandies themselves, as Father collected them for their early walk on a run where no cat ever escaped death. We heard Father shouting and all ran out in our night-clothes to try to separate the dogs, by carrying them together to the water-butt where one would let go.

Only one house overlooked the garden, and that was the Newland Arms kept by Mrs Capel. As the fight progressed we heard her shouting. 'Come on up, everyone, and see them Oakeleys in a dog fight.'

Each day after the dogs had been exercised we had Family Prayers. The maids all came in, and woe betide anyone who was late, usually a fine of sixpence. Father would read a piece from the Bible, and then we knelt for prayers, sniffing all the time to find out what was steaming away under the covers on the sideboard. On one occasion, Maggie, the new maid did not turn up and Father asked where she was.

'Maggie doesn't come to prayers, sir,' said the cook.

'Then Maggie packs her bags and goes after breakfast,' answered my Father, and she did.

Once my brother, Rowland, usually the quiet and docile member of the family, greatly daring planted a large moon daisy on the lawn outside the dining-room window. Father had always prided himself on his weedless lawns and spent long hours with a daisy picker extracting them. Suddenly we heard him stop in the middle of the Lord's Prayer, but it was only a short falter and vengeance waited until after the blessing.

By the time I was eight, Miss Swan could teach me no more and it was decided I must have a governess. A shy young woman with no qualifications at all was engaged to teach me and Peggy, the only other girl of my age in the village. We certainly led the poor girl a dance! Most of it was because we were anxious to learn and she could not teach us. We went for long walks collecting flowers, and pressed them on return, but if it had not been for my father reading me Dickens, Scott, Bulldog Drummond and Sherlock Holmes, I should have been very badly educated.

For holidays we went to Swanage with Nurse when we were little, and in later years when I saw parents enjoying the seaside with their little children, I thought what a lot our parents had missed. Later we went for holidays in a boat on the Thames, Father and Rowland rowing, Mother steering, and me looking after the dogs in the stern. When we tied up, we put up a tent, and I was allowed to practise rowing in an anchored boat. When the tent was up, Mother, Rowland and I slept in it, while Father shared the boat with the dogs. It always seemed to rain on these holidays and there were long dismal stretches when we huddled in mackintoshes, as Father rowed steadily on. Only once did he give way, when after a long and particularly cold and wet row we were allowed to spend the night at the Malster and Shovel in Moulsford. As we grew older we sometimes went to Brittany, ostensibly to learn French, but usually we found some English children and played with them. Eventually these holidays were given up because we were so difficult over the food!

One wonders if modern children with their dependence on television and the constant pursuit of excitement were as happy as our childhood when we had to make our own amusements – playing Old Maid with the maids in the kitchen; looking after the dolls; and gathering blackberries for the jam. At one time I organised a Gardeners' Guild for the magazine *Little Folks*, when we grew vegetables in our gardens and sold them to our parents so we could give money to the Cot Fund. Certainly, apart from a slight upset when my sister told me I was adopted (which was untrue) and I cried for days, my childhood was very happy.

However my childhood was to end abruptly. In December 1923 we had our annual children's party at The Gables. One of the guests was a child called Catherine, of whom I was very fond, though I disliked her mother, a large rather over bearing woman.

As we went up to Mother's bedroom to get everyone's coats, Catherine's Mother came up to me and said, 'Oh, hello Mary, I hear you are going away to boarding school.'

I was quite furious with Catherine's Mother for telling me first; furious with my Mother for not telling me first; and furious with myself because I thought I was going to cry at the thought.

'Oh, yes,' I replied, not wanting to let my Mother down, 'I did not think anyone knew. I am going away in the summer.'

As soon as the guests had gone I tackled my Mother.

'Oh, well,' she said, 'I was going to tell you tomorrow anyway. It is not quite settled. You could go as a day girl to Wychwood in Oxford if you like, or as a boarder to St John's, Bexhill where Rosemary's friends went. You can choose which you like.'

I made a hasty decision. 'I'll go to Bexhill,' I said, although I did not really want to leave home. Apparently my parents felt my governess could no longer either control or teach me properly, which was true. My Father actually disapproved of girls going away to school, and Rosemary had a governess until she was sixteen, but there seemed nothing for it, but to send me away.

In many ways I was excited. There would be proper teachers, and I should learn a whole lot of exciting new things; there would be lots of girls my own age with whom I could make friends; and there would be splendid games of hockey, tennis and netball. All this would make up for my somewhat lonely childhood.

So Mother and I went to Gorringe's to buy brown tunics, brown dresses, brown hats, brown shoes and stockings, and she embroidered my linen and shoe bags with my initials, and kind friends gave me presents to comfort me.

So on a dreary January morning I donned my new uniform, had my photo taken, kissed my dog Jilly and leaving childhood behind went off to be a schoolgirl.

ST JOHN'S

Chapter 2

Schooldays

All I knew about St John's School, Bexhill was that it was run by Miss Hamilton, the third generation of her family, who had run the school since 1820. My Parents had never visited it so could not tell me anything about it, and when I was there they usually just came to visit me once a year in the summer term.

I soon learned that the Headmistress was known as Miss Ham. My Mother took me to Charing Cross Station, and handed me over to her. She was a very large overpowering lady in a big hat, who immediately shepherded me into the train and allowed me to sit opposite her. After a short time the train started and I had a last glimpse of Mother standing on the platform with tears in her eyes, waving goodbye.

At Tunbridge Wells the train stopped and an Old Girl of the school arrived with a hamper of tea and cakes for Miss Ham. As a new girl I was honoured with a sandwich to the envy of the other occupants of the carriage.

On arrival at Bexhill, we got in a bus which took us to Little St John's, the junior house which was just across the road from the main building. On arrival I was greeted by the Matron, Miss Martin.

'Oh, you're the little girl who has just had her appendix out. I will take you to lie down straight away.'

I replied indignantly that I still had my appendix and the other new girl, Nancy, was duly found and taken off. I was then shown my dormitory, and immediately received a very hostile greeting.

'We don't want you here,' they said. 'You've spoilt everything by coming in the spring term. We were all best friends in this dormitory and now Hazel has been moved to another dormitory and we've got a horrible new girl instead.'

From then on the teasing never stopped. Everything I said was misconstrued; my clothes were all wrong, particularly my white Sunday coat, which had been my sister's, and was slightly yellow; and my time in that dormitory was sheer misery.

In school I was not particularly happy either. The first Sunday we had to learn the Collect by heart, and after five minutes I put up my hand to say I had learnt it. This did not endear me to my fellows who were just about to find where it was in the Prayer Book. In addition, because the Form of my age group was full, I was put with the younger girls in Form Two. I came top the first week and since there were never any moves up or down, simply the addition of a few new girls as the years went by, I remained top for the whole of my school career. I was a child who flourished on competition and so I rapidly became bored and spent long hours in preparation writing letters or novels because I had finished my work too quickly.

Little St John's was run by a Housemistress Miss Copley who was a splendid teacher, and Miss Martin or Marty as we called her, the Matron. I loved Miss Copley's history lessons most of which were about the Greeks and the Romans. Years later when I was a Headmistress, I was asked to go and see her where she lay dying of cancer in a nursing home. Her sister told me Miss Copley was worrying about something and asked me to help.

'My dear,' she whispered, 'I am so unhappy. All these years of teaching and I took so much trouble, and thought I gave so much to the children at St John's, but now I am beginning to think it was all useless and they learnt nothing and could not recite anything I taught them.'

There was a long pause and then I turned to her, 'Miss Copley,' I said, 'listen and I will recite for you the Books of the Bible – the Roman Emperors, and the names of Shakespeare's plays,' and I did.

'My dear,' came a voice I could hardly hear, 'I am happy, I did teach someone. Now I can go in peace knowing my long teaching career was not in vain.'

The terror of Little St John's was Marty the Matron who descended on us every Friday night while we were having our baths with a large spoonful of Syrup of Figs. I was always terrified of getting into her sick-room but managed to avoid it. By the end of my time at Little St John's I was much happier because I had a friend called Mollie who spent most of her time drawing dogs, but when I went up to the senior school she was left behind as she was younger than me.

St John's was a very family school. Most of the girls were the daughters of service people or from the business world. Ham was a kind of substitute mother and called us all her Dearies. Each Thursday night she visited the dormitories, gave us each a large wet kiss, and a bar of chocolate, instructing us to be sure to clean our teeth afterwards, Three times a term

Staff meetings were held and a list of offenders was read out. Each of them had to go to Miss Ham's study and I was usually on it. Sometimes it was for being conceited over my work: others for having untidy hair or not trying at games. We were made to sit on a low stool and listen to the complaints. Each Saturday morning at prayers we were all asked if we had talked after lights out and there was much discussion as to what was meant by 'talking'.

'I only said one word – I just said "goodnight" – I only talked in deaf and dumb language,' and so on. So we stayed sitting and suffered the pangs of conscience afterwards.

My main problem was that I could not make friends. No one liked the clever girls and in addition I was hopeless at games and a plain little girl, the smallest in the form.

In our free time we sat in the play-room. In one corner sat the 'Fast Set' who went to dances and theatres in the holidays; in the other sat the 'Goodies' doing their needlework and swotting up their work; and in the middle alone at a table reading her history novel sat Mary Oakeley by herself, wishing she could be invited to one or the other, but secretly feeling she would not fit into either.

However one term there appeared a very attractive new girl called Yvonne, and I decided I wanted her for my best friend. I was told I had no hope!

'What! A grubby little swot like you,' the others jeered. 'She does marvellous paintings. Her Mother's an artist, and her Father is Managing Director of one of the big newspapers. She'd just laugh if you asked her to be your best friend.'

But she did not. I laid my plans well. I saw she loved to be amused and coming from a home where there was always sparkling and witty conversation she was bored with schoolgirls giggling. I managed to get her as my partner on a crocodile walk and set out to be as witty and amusing as I could. Fascinated, she asked me to walk with her again and the friendship was sealed. It lasted throughout her marriage (bridesmaid); her children (godmother); and many happy visits to the homes of her parents and herself.

Very little was done to amuse us in our spare time at St John's. We sometimes had a Rin Tin Tin film on a Saturday evening, and it was a special punishment to miss the first quarter of an hour, which was annoying. We were only allowed out for walks in crocodile and the only interesting one was the one on Sunday called the 'Advertisement Walk', when clad in our best white coats and skirts we paraded along the Bexhill

Front. The great excitement was the Bexhill Rowing Club, a group of lusty young men sunning themselves about half-way along. But, alas, as soon as we reached them, Ham sent a small girl up to the top to tell the crocodile to turn. As the runner went she was admonished to 'Go Slow' so we might get a peep, at least.

We had to make our own amusements. Occasionally we were allowed to act plays or charades. but as we were forbidden to wear trousers it became difficult always to have characters in jodhpurs or butcher's aprons. I gained some notoriety as the inventor of the 'Bedroom Game'. We always had to take our Bibles to bed, and there was a five minute silence for Bible reading and prayers. Ours was a very noisy dormitory but when the Matron came round we were always reading our Bibles.

The game consisted of the leader calling out a Bible reference, and everyone had to find it. Whoever found it first had to 'worship the Lord' or 'clap your hands' or 'kneel down and pray'. The winner got a point, and the Matrons never found out what was going on. We were just studying our Bibles, we announced, trying to look holy.

On Sunday nights the Matrons all went over to have supper with Ham in the main building, and those of us who slept in the annexe called the Lodge had a fine old time, putting mattresses on the stairs to come down the Cresta Run; playing hide and seek in the lavatories; and visiting Matron's bedroom and trying on her hats!

At one stage, Yvonne and I were sleeping in the main school which was immediately above the dining-room where Ham entertained her Sunday night guests. One Sunday night the fire engine went by, and Yvonne leapt out of bed to see it. In doing so she upset the slop pail containing our dirty washing water and to our horror we realised it was seeping through the floor into the dining-room beneath. As we anticipated, it was not long before a flurry of angry Matrons descended on us and scolded us as they mopped the floor. Never had we laughed so much though we managed to keep straight faces every time the Matrons looked up.

Ham believed in the punishment fitting the crime. I suffered once when I was fed up with the girl who sat next to me in prep. I threw a ball of paper at her but unfortunately hit the staff taking prep full in the face. Needless to say I was sent straight to Miss Ham's study.

'It's disgraceful,' she remarked, 'a girl of fourteen cannot hit a target at which she is aiming. Come to prayers tonight with six tennis balls and a waste-paper basket, and learn to aim straight.'

I duly obeyed and while the whole school was champing to get to their free time, I tried unsuccessfully to get the balls into the basket. I was so embarrassed they went everywhere and it took nearly a quarter of an hour to get them all in. I never threw balls of paper at anyone again; and Joan never sang on a walk again after she had to sing before the whole school at prayers.

Gradually I moved up the school. I learnt to play tennis, but of course we were not allowed to stand with our feet apart because it was unladylike. I became quite good at hockey and actually played centre half in the second eleven; I passed my Junior and Senior Cambridge Examinations, and found myself being first a Prefect, and then Head Girl with the juniors having pashes on me. I put my hair up and felt very grown up, though in actual fact we were kept very much as children.

For many years I had noticed a little house away on the hill opposite the school. As Prefects we were allowed to go for walks in threes and one day we set off to find the house. Unfortunately it was further than we thought and after had found it, we got lost and came back through the outskirts of the town which was strictly forbidden. Foolishly we felt sure someone in authority must have seen us or we had been missed, so we went to confess to Ham. There was the most tremendous row and we all thought we would be expelled. In the end it all died down but we were out of favour for the rest of the term.

Academically, my last year was a fiasco. I had decided I wanted to go to Oxford but none of the Staff at St John's except Ham herself had ever been there. Most of the Staff had not even been to a University. I was told it was quite impossible and I must think of something else. As I persisted a retired lady Missionary, who lived in Bexhill, was brought in to teach me. I soon found out I knew more than she did, and most of us in the Sixth Form were equally bored. Our only interest was in the newly founded library, which was full of interesting medical books left by an elderly cousin of Ham. As our knowledge of the facts of life was practically nil, we improved our knowledge in this area at least.

Yvonne had left and our Sixth Form was enlivened by one Curly who got into every possible kind of mischief. Once being in a rage with me she threw ink all over my Sunday cushion which my grandmother had embroidered for me and, in consequence of someone telling, the Matron had to spend all her free time in their sitting room embroidering a new one. On another occasion having quarrelled with her best friend they made it up with a long embrace after lights, only for the best friend to find the seat of her pyjamas had been cut out. On another occasion the school potted plants were all given a chemical solution with astonishing results. Without Curly our last year would have been dull indeed!

And so schooldays came to an end. We had our 100th anniversary of the founding of the school by Ham's great aunt, when we all danced in crinolines before our assembled Parents who were making their annual visit; we said goodbye and gave leaving presents to the Staff, hoping we would not grow up like them. We had fond kisses with all our friends and signed ourselves up as Old Girls in perpetuity.

Finally, we all went solemnly to Ham's drawing-room for our farewell talk. Years later I talked to groups of leaving girls, but my advice was very different from hers! All I can remember of that memorable scene was Ham saying very fiercely: 'Dearies, please remember not to let silly boys kiss you.'

In those days I was not sure if kissing led to babies so I took careful note!

We had a last kiss from Ham, who had promised to take us to see *Cavalcade* as a parting treat. The following day we were on a train bound for Charing Cross where it had all begun ten years before. Now we were poised for an exciting new life far from Bexhill's western slopes.

As we neared London the more daring took off their flower-pot hats, and threw them out of the window. The rest of us kept them for the next rummage sale.

OXFORD

Chapter 3

Oxford Days

All my life I had wanted to go to Oxford. Living only six miles away, I had visited most of the colleges, been to the Encaenia and enjoyed undergraduates coming to tea on Sunday at The Gables. Yet how was I to get there? The numbers of women applying was strictly limited, and there were many other applications for very few places. Strangely enough my Mother was very against me trying for Oxford, but my father, whose distinguished cousin Dr Hilda Oakeley had been at Somerville and was later Principal of Victoria College in Canada was all in favour.

My Mother managed to get an introduction to Miss Burrows whose mother had been the first Principal of St Hilda's and it was decided to seek her advice. Unfortunately, when we went to call Miss Burrows was moving house and we were only able to converse in a bare room with the removal men working all round us, so it was a somewhat hurried conversation.

'I am against my daughter going to Oxford,' said my Mother. 'What do you think, Miss Burrows?'

Miss Burrows gave a searching look at me and after a long pause replied, 'I don't really think she is at all suitable. It is very difficult for girls from small private schools to get in to Oxford, and she looks very young and childish.'

Years later when I sat next to Miss Burrows at a dinner at St Hilda's I reminded her of this conversation. When she heard of my subsequent career she was a little taken aback!

In spite of Miss Burrows' advice my Father let me push on and sent me to Mrs Lobel, a well-known history coach, and to an elderly gentleman who lived in Wellington Square to see if he could get some Latin into my head. For the first time, when I went to Mrs Lobel, I was up against someone who could really teach and I enjoyed every minute of my coachings. I soon realised how little I knew, and how poor were my essays, and I knew from the look on Mrs Lobel's face she thought I had little chance of getting in.

Nevertheless I plodded on and took the Entrance Examination for Lady Margaret Hall. The Principal, Miss Linda Grier was reputed to be very fond of playing tenniquoit and I practised for long hours in the hope I might gain her favour by my prowess. But it was not to be. Although I got an interview I realised when I was surrounded by candidates from Roedean, Wycombe Abbey and Cheltenham Ladies College how little I knew. There was even a girl from St Felix, Southwold and I confessed to her I had once longed to go to that school after happy holidays with my Grandmother, who had a holiday house in Southwold. But my Father thought it was too far away and too expensive.

The result was inevitable and a rejection slip landed on my breakfast table a few weeks later. The only consolation was that I was on the waiting list. I think my Mother was secretly pleased, and I spent the summer 'doing the Season', going to the Eton and Harrow Match, to Eights Week, to a Commem Ball, to Henley and the Derby. Each day I scanned the post for a letter from Lady Margaret but none came and in my heart of hearts I knew it was hopeless.

Then one morning there was a typed letter from Oxford but it was not from Lady Margaret Hall but from St Hilda's, saying they were short of history candidates and were calling up those on Lady Margaret Hall's waiting list. Would I come for an interview as soon as possible?

Calling out the good news to my family, I left the breakfast table, got on my bicycle and biked into Oxford as fast as I could go. I arrived at St Hilda's just before nine and went straight into the dining-room where the dons were having breakfast.

The Principal, Miss Julia de Lacy Mann looked up in some surprise. 'Who are you?' she asked, rather taken aback.

'I've come about the history place,' I replied blushing furiously.

'Have you had any breakfast?' she inquired, and when I said I had not I was invited to sit down and have some. Then Miss Sandys, the Senior History Don took me over to her room and the interview began. I told her how desperately I wanted to come to Oxford and she asked me to criticise her pictures.

I knew nothing about art, and I gazed at Van Gogh's *Cornfields* and wondered what to say. Then I remembered how bored we had all got with my sister, Rosemary always talking about her art lessons and how important it was to get good composition into a picture.

'It has excellent composition,' I volunteered.

Miss Sandys was delighted and a few days later I got a note to say I had been accepted for a History Place for September 1932. Rosemary always maintained she got me into Oxford and I had to buy her a Yoyo, which were all the craze at the time, to placate her.

Unfortunately, St Hilda's were building a new block on the end of Hall, and two students had to live out during their first year. As I was the bottom of everyone I had to live in lodgings in Park Town which was the other end of Oxford, and so a total disaster. I was too shy to go out on my bike to Drama Societies or other meetings, and as there was no one I knew at college, I made no friends, the lodgings were very overcrowded and the food very meagre. There was only one bathroom for eight people, which included two men, and I used to drop in at Ellistons to wash on my way to St Hilda's. If I had not been near home, and able to go there every Sunday, life would have been bleak indeed.

But the highlight of that first year was the teaching. Few history tutors could have been so stimulating or interesting as Miss Sandys. From her I gained a deep love of history and her tutorials were the highlight of the week.

At first I was the weak one in the group, but under the guidance of Miss Sandys, I scraped through Pass Mods, having the good fortune to have a Latin Unseen I had done before. So I was able to go on to study sixteenth-century European history with David Keir, then at University College and later Master of Balliol. There were fascinating days sitting in Duke Humphrey looking at manuscripts, and later when I took Indian history as a special subject, enjoying the delights of the Indian Institute. My great great-grandfather, Sir Charles Oakeley had been Governor of Madras in the time of Tippu Sahib, so I had a special interest in Indian history, which I studied with Sir Geoffrey Corbett.

Yet Oxford was not all work. I was sad to see so many students who spent all their time studying and so not getting the best out of university life. There were college dances when we daringly laced the lemonade with gin; long hours drifting in a punt on the Cherwell with the latest boyfriend; the hectic love affairs; and the lure of Shotover and Wytham. I went on with my hockey and even once filled in a vacancy in the University team. Nine terms seemed all too short.

It was an age when undergraduates were very politically minded and we went from the Labour Club to the Conservatives; to the October Club and the Union, where the fateful debate on King and Country took place. On one occasion the Red Flag actually flew over St Hilda's on Empire Day as we had a group of very Left students. Most of us wanted to see the world put to rights!

Certainly life was easier and happier when I moved into College in my second year, but the making of college friends remained at first. As at school there was the rich set coming from the big public schools and the poorer scholarship girls from the grammar schools. Since the student who shared my history tutorial was in the former I sat with them at meals but received a rude shock when one of them came into my room one evening.

'I'm afraid I'm going to be brutal and say we don't want you in our set,' she began. 'You see, we are all from the well-known girls' public schools and you are an outsider from a small private one; you were not in College when we made our friends; and we've heard your Father is a Liberal which puts you quite beyond the pale.'

So that was that. In future I sat with a miner's daughter from South Wales and found most of my friends outside College. One of these was known as Horse, though she really had the very attractive name of Rowan, and was a home student. I first met her at a foundation meeting of the Women's Debating Society, when we caught each other's eye during a particularly boring speech. From then on, until her premature death from tuberculosis, she was a devoted friend and made her mark first as a solicitor and later as a clergyman's wife.

It was at this debating society I made my maiden speech on 'Life is just a bowl of cherries'. I was immensely proud of it until I got back to St Hilda's and heard someone say: 'Who was it made that frightful speech tonight? Not someone from this College I hope.'

Half-way through my second year came the election of the JCR officers. I had always attended the meetings and admired the outgoing President who had been one of the most successful the College had had. In our year there was an outstanding candidate, and there was little interest in the election. Imagine my surprise when on coming down to breakfast I saw a notice on the Principal's notice board, 'Mary Oakeley has been elected President of the JCR'.

Everyone was astonished. My tutor said, 'You are a dark horse!' and I could not get over it when everyone came to congratulate me. It seemed the rich set, ashamed of their behaviour to me, had backed me strongly. For me it was one of the highlights of my life. Headmistresses and Head girls are chosen by others on their merits but a JCR president is chosen by her contemporaries and my appointment made up for earlier disappointments at Oxford. It meant I had first choice of all the college rooms in my third year, and I chose a large room in Hall which had been the Chapel, and had a glorious view over Christchurch Meadow and Merton.

Being President meant meetings with college Principals, chairing meetings, and representing the college at various functions. It was during this time that we gained the exciting privilege of being allowed to have men in our rooms for tea, provided they were out of the college by 7 p.m.!

It was in my second year that I was invited to go to Canon Bryan Green's Bible classes in Blackhall Road. I think we were all in love with him and sat adoringly at his feet while he expounded the Epistle to the Romans. Later he planned a Mission to Coventry and invited me to go. The idea was that all the Coventry clergy should go on holiday and the students would take over. I was keen to go but my Mother was worried and wrote to Canon Cragg who was one of the organisers saying she felt I was too young and unsophisticated for this sort of thing! If I was, it was my family's fault as no one ever told me the facts of life and when I upbraided my Mother about it, all she said was, 'I took it for granted you knew.'

Coventry was certainly an eye opener to me. For the first week I stayed with an elderly couple. The husband was a bank clerk and was paid £2 a week. On Sunday we had a joint, and the rest of the week it was hotted up. The bath was literally full of geraniums; there was only cold water and an outside lavatory shared with the house next door. The second week I stayed with a young Air Force couple who lived in a new council house and it was much more comfortable.

We were in the Parish of St Margaret's, but also visited a mining village on the outskirts of Coventry. We spoke to Mothers' Unions, Girl Guides and GFS groups; visited round the parishes; and helped in the churches. Perhaps the most difficult task was speaking in factory canteens when the men were all playing cards, and no one seemed to be listening. Every day there was a formal meeting for all the students, when we reported what we had done. I became rather depressed, as no one seemed to come and ask me for advice, and then suddenly I had my chance.

'Has anyone had any particular problems?' asked Bryan Green as usual.

'Yes, I have,' I answered proudly.

Canon Green looked surprised but he asked me to continue.

'There is a woman in the parish who is very unhappy,' I began. 'She came to tell me she cannot get on with her husband who ill treats her. She is considering going off with her lodger.'

'And what did you advise?' asked Canon Green.

'That she should certainly go off with the lodger,' I answered.

There was consternation. I was asked the address, and one of the Mirfield Fathers was sent off on his bicycle to put the matter right. Years later Canon Green and I laughed about this episode which he never let me forget. However, I was invited to preach in the old Coventry Cathedral at Harvest Festival, when somewhat oddly the subject was the Jewish people about whom I fortunately had just bought a new Penguin. I often thought of this in later years as I wandered round the new cathedral.

But Oxford was not all study, and I used to look forward to Sundays when I biked back to The Gables and was met by the current bevy of boyfriends. There was Trevor Huddleston, later to work in South Africa; the Russell brothers who were both killed in Malaya; Robert and Lionel whom I had met on a cruise in Norway; and a group of New Zealanders. Of them all, Jack Bromley was the most brilliant, and I remember how in the war he was travelling by Tube and left an important Home Office set of papers behind, with disastrous results.

Unlike nowadays when students roam the Continent, I stayed in the vacations with my relations in various parts of England and Scotland or accompanied my parents on cruises which suited my Father who was already crippled with arthritis.

It was on one of the cruises that I met Arnold, who was there with his Father and Mother. He became very attached to me, and I later went to stay with the family in Sussex. Both sets of parents took it for granted we would be engaged before I left Oxford, and it seems strange nowadays to say I still had no idea exactly what marriage involved.

Back in Oxford for my second year I was duly surprised when a handsome fair-haired young man came up after a lecture and invited me to go out with him that evening. I could hardly believe it that I, the ugly duckling, had attracted someone so handsome!

This was the beginning of the typical Oxford love-affair. Happy days punting on the river; teas in New College; dances in the Carfax Assembly Rooms; and very little work done at all. Finally, I wrote to Arnold and told him any engagement was off. The highlight was the Commem Ball. I had been in my first year with one of my brother's friends, but this was with Donald. I persuaded my Mother to give me a new dress, of pink net, and with a special hair-do, I sat in College for Donald to fetch me.

But he never came. It was nine o'clock . . . ten . . . eleven . . . twelve and at one I went to bed in tears, and the pink dress lay on the floor.

Next morning was a Sunday, and I went to The Gables as usual. As we walked round the gardens, Jack Bromley said to me: 'Did you hear about the troubles at New College last night? One of the students got thrown out of the window by a Communist group and broke his back?'

My Mother realised something had happened and took me into the house. Next day I heard Donald was alive but in a private nursing home.

Several days later I went to see him lying on sandbags, unable to move. I knew he was planning to go into the Army. This would now be impossible and, later I knew, so was any idea of marriage. In actual fact he did partially recover, thanks to a brilliant international surgeon, did get called up, and was killed almost immediately. I still look at the Board of Remembrance when I go showing visitors round New College.

This I felt was my unlucky year because in the summer vacation I fell ill with scarlet fever, and nearly died. Unfortunately, I gave it to my Father but he had it only slightly.

Back in Oxford for my last year. I was determined to get a good degree and settled down to hard work. My tutor, now Mrs Leys told me I should get a good third if I was lucky but a fourth if I was not. The Schools' Week was incredibly hot, and I was bitterly disappointed that the eighteenth-century paper was full of military and naval history, about which I knew nothing. However, the paper on Indian history was a delight and I was glad I had learnt so much about my ancestor.

To my delight I got a Viva, and appeared before a group of eminent historians. I seemed to get on well as we discussed the vagaries of Catherine de Medici, but worse was to come.

'Miss Oakeley,' the Chairman continued, 'you seem a little unsure

Graduation Day

27

about Medieval Europe. Your answers on the geography of this region seem to show a lack of knowledge.'

My heart sank as I thought of that terrible patchwork of bishoprics, electorates, and empires scattered over the map of Europe.

'I'm sorry,' I remarked, 'if I appeared not to understand it, as I have a really good idea of it.'

To my horror a large sheet of paper was produced, a black pencil was laid on it, and I was invited to draw a map of Europe at the Treaty of Westphalia. At first I got on well. I sketched in the Holy Roman Empire, added a few bishoprics, and encircled the Electorate of Hanover.

'Perhaps, Miss Oakeley,' the voice went on, 'you would put in the ports, particularly those of northern Europe, since Bremen and Verden play such a part in the history of this period. The course of the Rhine and the port of Hamburg.'

In went the Rhine, fortunately finding its way to the sea in Holland; Bremen and Verden followed – somewhere near their right places; but where was Hamburg? East or west of Denmark?

'And Hamburg,' the voice went on relentlessly.

I hesitated, sent up a prayer and put it east of Denmark. I could hear the sighs of disappointment but in spite of this I got a top second and just missed a first. I was top of St Hilda's history candidates of whom there were only a few but my Father always upbraided me about Hamburg, and said I had lost my first because of my stupidity!

So Oxford days came to an end. Mrs Leys surprised at my success wanted me to stay another year and do a B Litt but my Father put his foot down. In those days there were no grants except university scholarships and for three years he had provided £200 a year for my education. As college and university fees were £150, I had £50 a year for clothes, books, travelling etc. If it had not been for my Mother's surreptitious generosity and Christmas tips I should have been in great troubles. I still look back to the days when I cashed a cheque for £1 and wondered if I was overdrawn, or watched two of the other students pawning some silver candlesticks left them by their aunt to meet their fees.

I went to the Sheldonian to take my BA Degree and proudly wore my white fur hood, and gave the right responses in Latin, obeyed the message we got from the Vice-Chancellor that we would not be accepted if we wore lipstick! After that it meant looking for a job. I had really hoped to get married when I finished but when my New College friend was thrown out of his window and broke his back, this was not realistic and I had to think again.

ST JAMES'S

Chapter 4

St James's: West Malvern

While I was wondering what I should do next, the phone went and it was Miss Alice Baird, Headmistress of St James's, West Malvern asking me if I would consider coming to teach history in her school. There were six famous Miss Bairds, all over six feet tall, and between them they had founded three different schools, St James's, Abbots Hill and Evendine. They must have been formidable to grumbling parents!

Since there was no other job in sight, I went over for an interview in Miss Alice's beautiful drawing-room, graced with a large photograph of her ex-pupil the Duchess of Gloucester. After a short interview I found myself appointed to teach history and geography in a school of 220 girls, at a princely salary of £135 a year. I had had no teachers' training, and my only experience was a rather disastrous one in the Eynsham Sunday School, when a boy put a firework under my chair and I sent him home to the dismay of the Vicar who had been imploring his Mother to send him for several weeks!

So when September came, off I went and found myself living in Church Cottage with the gym mistress and the art specialist. I had to work every day with a half-day on the Saturday provided there were no matches. I shall never forget my first lesson which was 2b geography and I waited in trepidation, but when the class came there were only three girls and we were soon talking of Norway where I had spent my summer holiday.

St James's was organised on the Dalton System. Each member of Staff had to prepare a monthly assignment of work for each girl and I was most fortunate in having the ones from the year before left for me to copy. I had a tin hut in the garden as my class-room and here the girls came to do their assignments when they felt like it. Some who liked me spent most of the month in my room: those who did not refused to come unless I hunted for them round the school and brought them in.

Each week I had to ask each girl individually about her work; look at any maps and drawings she might have done; and correct her essays. When finished the work was crossed off on a card, and those with everything crossed off at the end of the month had a day's holiday. Those not finished had to work and there were always long queues at the Maths and French rooms, though it was possible to go through one's whole school career without doing either.

I soon learnt the technique of fetching people to do my subjects early in the month but it was hard work, and I remember an Egyptian girl who was on a special diet sent down each day from Fortnum and Mason, being found in the cloakroom eating a large pork pie bought via the gardener's boy and bringing her, pork pie and all, to my room to do some history.

The system meant my being in my room from nine till one; and again from five until seven each day. In between I had to take hockey every afternoon and was on duty every Sunday to take the girls to church or walk. On Saturday morning we had our rooms open from nine until twelve-thirty. Soon I was asked to take Economics, Psychology and Current Events with the Sixth Form. Needless to say I knew nothing about these subjects and had to learn them up before each lesson. On Monday I had to give a Current Events lesson to the whole school, so in term time I never seemed to have any time off, especially as we had to sit with the girls at meals and make polite conversation.

Life in the Staff room took some getting used to and I blotted my copybook soon after my arrival. A new cupboard was brought into the Staff room and it turned out to be different from the original one I had noticed. The other junior member of Staff, one O'Rorke and I were in the Staff room at the time and we chose our shelves with care. I labelled mine 'MO. Keep off'.

However, we had been misinformed. It had been in the Staff room before and had gone away to be painted. When the senior mistress came in, she went very red in the face.

'Miss Oakeley,' she said, turning to me, 'I have been here seventeen years, and I have always kept my books on a certain shelf in the Staff room, but when I came to put them in their usual place I find a piece of paper labelled "MO. Keep off". Kindly remove it at once.' – Which I did.

Because we were the two junior members of Staff, O'Rorke and I got all the odd jobs.

'I know it is a wet afternoon and there is no hockey, but I want to have my hair done, so perhaps one of you would take games in the gym.'

'The matron has had a fall. Would one of you supervise putting to bed tonight, please?'

'The Art Mistress is ill. I'm afraid one of you must give up your

Saturday afternoon, and sit in the art room.'

We never thought of striking, and we had not heard of the NUT, so meekly did what we were asked, though we got the reputation of being cheeky since we sometimes found a good excuse. O'Rorke taught Science and her lab was near my room, so we became friends especially after she nearly blew her eyebrows off in an experiment, and I went to the rescue. She had taught in Burma, and had a small car so we sometimes with great daring escaped to the pictures in Worcester in the evening, and once went to the Aldershot Tattoo, driving all night and walking in to take our classes, yawning heavily at 9 a.m.

Miss Alice was eighty at the time but she still had her school under control. She only had to say: 'My dears, I don't like it, please do not do it again,' and they did not.

One time I was particulary angry about something and announced, in the Staff Room, 'I shall go and see Miss Alice and see if she can put it right.'

Greatly daring I went round to the holy of holies and knocked on the door.

When I went in, Miss Alice was sitting writing, but she looked up and smiled. 'Ah, Miss Oakeley, I did so want to see you. Someone told me your Mother was not well. How is she?'

This conversation went on for some time, and continued with further inquiries about my sister, Rosemary who had been at Evendine with Miss Georgina. By the time she asked me if I had anything special to say, I had cooled down and simply said I had come about a matter which no doubt the senior mistress could sort out, and sailed back to the Staff Room. The other Staff merely smiled on my return as most of them had had the same experience.

Discipline consisted of a series of slips; pink ones called Recommendations and blue ones called Vetoes, which were read out at prayers. Miss Alice was always late for prayers and the Staff waited outside the hall, sometimes for twenty minutes. Most of the girls disliked the French mademoiselle, and one morning they stuck pins under her chair with the points sticking up. Unfortunately there was a visitor sitting with the Staff that morning and we were all moved one along. I found myself sitting on the pins as the lesson was read, and praying as we knelt down that Miss Alice would not ask us to sit again for notices.

St James's had wide and extensive grounds with beautiful trees and a stupendous view over Wales. The Staff had to patrol the grounds at the weekends in case any boyfriends had slipped in. There was also a lovely swimming pool which I got to know well. For a week at the end of term I was deputed to sleep on a camp bed beside it, as there were rumours that midnight swimming was on the agenda.

Perhaps the most interesting event during my time at St James's was taking the Sixth Form to Ashridge. How I was ever allowed to do this still amazes me! At that time it was a Conservative College which ran weekend and weekly courses in current affairs. I would set off with some twenty Sixth Formers in mufti, make-up hurriedly applied in the train, right across London, stopping to see the Houses of Parliament or the Mint, and arriving at Ashridge late on Friday evening.

From then on it was very difficult to keep track of the girls, as there was always a lot of handsome young men on the courses, so I eventually gave it up and apart from rounding up the girls to go to bed, I enjoyed myself. We met all sorts of interesting people including Unity Mitford, fresh from meeting Hitler, and telling us what a charming man he was and showing us the Swastika badge he had given her.

Once on the way back I nearly landed in trouble. One of the girls was a very bad traveller and was so sick on the train, I thought she was going to pass out. I hurried along to the dining-car and got a glass of neat brandy which I gave to her. The result was we had to help her off the train and she was quite unfit to go back to school where Miss Alice was waiting to hear all about their adventures.

Fortunately, I was friendly with the Nursing Sister and the Sanatorium was on the way back to school so I stopped there and explained that I had inadvertently made one of the party inebriated, and left her there to recover in peace. On Miss Alice's inquiries I explained the girl had been taken ill on the train and I had handed her over to Sister.

The first year of teaching is following in someone else's footsteps; the second you are getting into your stride; and the third you are really on your own. By the end of three years at St James's I felt I needed a change. I had only been in trouble once, and that had passed over quickly. One of the Staff at St James's was engaged to one of the masters at a boys' school and I think she was rather annoyed that through an introduction I was invited there too. At the dinner party were two young men. To my surprise one, Richard, seemed to know my family well, and turned out to be a second cousin, and later he took me for wonderful walks all over the countryside whenever I could get off.

The other was Charles, the son of a prominent MP and when we were due to go home, and the Spanish girl had reluctantly offered to take me back to St James's in her fiancé's car, Charles handed me into the open dicky and jumped in too.

When we got to St James's the Spanish girl turned to me and said, 'I hope you were not cold in that dicky.'

Since Charles and I had been tightly locked together under his coat, I foolishly replied, 'Oh no, we were as warm as anything.'

The next morning I was sent for to Miss Alice's study and told she was shocked to hear of my behaviour after the Headmaster's dinner party. Charles was also called up, and he, too, was reprimanded. I never saw him again in Malvern, but by a strange quirk of fate he turned up at a tennis party in New Zealand, married with three children. I said nothing!

Still, I was sad to leave St James's but three years in a first job was said to be enough. I had a bout of slight heart trouble from bounding over the gap in the Malvern Hills; O'Rorke had left to be married; and I felt I could not spend my whole life coping with the Dalton System. I shall always remember Miss Alice with great affection, and be grateful for all her guidance in my first job.

INTERLUDE

Chapter 5

Interlude

It was lovely to feel free again, and to be able to plan one's life, without being bound by a timetable. I felt I had done enough teaching and might try something else.

In the summer holidays we went on another cruise to Norway. I remember noticing a middle-aged woman, always dressed in black, who got off at a Fiord in the north. She was accompanied by the Purser and one of the other officers, and went off in a Police car. To our surprise, when she returned just before we sailed she was followed by two men carrying a coffin.

It appeared she had come here with her young husband on their honeymoon, and he had slipped and gone down a glacier. She had been told the time had come when his body would appear, still in his youth, and she could fetch it, which she did. It must have been a terrible experience for her.

In later years I was dubbed accident prone! It was on this cruise, when I was dressing for dinner on the last night a stream of water appeared over the door. A steward was summoned and he told me it was cold water, and I had better come out before the pipe burst altogether. I did but it was boiling water and my back was burnt all the way down. I rushed to my parents' cabin. My Mother said,' 'You can't come in, your Father has not got his trousers on!'

As soon as he was dressed the Surgeon came and patched me up, but it was a terrible journey home and my Mother sent me down to my Grandmother in Southwold to recover. There I saw the school where I had wanted to be a pupil, and wished I had been. Little did I know what the future held!

One of my happiest times was spent with Yvonne and her family, and I had not been able to see much of them with my limited free time at St James's. It was a wonderful household with Jimmie Brown head of the Amalgamated Press; Sibyl, his wife a famous artist; Aunt Yvonne running the house and looking after the children; and Gerald, the little brother who had an important role to play in the house.

The Browns had many friends old and young. There were splendid tennis parties, when the older ones timidly served underhand, and happy dances when Gerald played the drums, and attractive young men were in great supply. After each dance there was a post-mortem on everyone's behaviour!

Jimmie Brown was concerned that I had no job. He was the kindest man, and whenever I was leaving Tudor House, he slipped a pound into my pocket, which was very welcome. Now he took me up to the Amalgamated Press where I was interviewed for a job on the women's pages, but it fell through as my Father would not let me live in London.

I was bridesmaid at Yvonne's wedding to Dr William Snell, a TB specialist. The marriage was in Hendon Church and we were glad when it was over, as the chief bridesmaid was suffering from appendicitis, and we did not know if she would get through, and the bride's father and the groom, not being churchgoers, caused the Almighty to send a terrific thunderstorm which drowned all the acceptances.

Still I had no job, and friends tried to make me take up nursing which I would have hated. Our friend Emily Macmannus, who was Matron of Guys, had me to stay but even she did not convince me.

Apart from everything else, money was getting short, and I was quite pleased when I got a phone call from the Headmistress of St George's, Ascot, asking me if I could possibly come for three weeks to teach history as her history mistress had got chicken pox. In spite of saying I would never teach again, I decided to go.

St George's was a very different type of school from St James's. The history mistress taught only history and there were lots of free periods, and adequate time off. As we were near London we were able to go to cinemas and theatres, meet our friends and go to parties. By this time I had a small car, and could get home quite easily. In fact all the time I was at Ascot I went home on Thursday evenings to take the Eynsham Brownies.

The Headmistress, Miss Loveday who had founded the school, was much younger than Miss Alice and a strict disciplinarian. The staff were all called by their surnames, and she walked the passages in school time looking through the glass partition in the class-room doors. Afterwards in the staff room, it was, 'Oakeley, I saw a girl fidgeting in your class. Do not let it happen again.'

It did not because I taught the girls that when a face was looking through the glass, I would move my inkpot to the other side and all must be still.

The Head had her favourites, and fortunately I was one. When the history mistress came back, I was asked to stay too, and we had a wonderful time dividing the lessons. We slept in an annexe. My friendly historian suffered from epilepsy, and when she screamed in the night I had to rush and smother her with a pillow. Yet all this time there was always the shadow of war, which had been postponed in 1938 and now looked very imminent. Miss Loveday was worried because the school was so near Sandhurst and Camberley. She arranged for large shelters to be built for any emergency, and told the Staff she had ordered special food from Fortnum and Mason so that the girls would not be frightened.

Then, of course, we had to have practices, and the girls and Staff all processed down, and examined the new home they would occupy when raids took place. 'And,' said Miss Loveday, the cupboards are full of special food from Fortnums so you can all have midnight feast while we are waiting.'

It was always difficult to find Miss Loveday, as the school had no drawing-room or Head's study. The only place you could find her was her bedroom, which was a most hazardous adventure. When you knocked on the door and she said, 'Come In,' (or you thought she did) she would say, 'Come in, come in, don't keep knocking. Didn't you hear me say "Come In"?' Or else you opened the door, went in, and found her in a state of undress!

Matches were very important events, especially the one against Downe House, St George's great rivals. Both Headmistresses were moved to tears by defeat, and next morning at Assembly at St George's colours were stripped off; the PE Staff were publicly reproved; and tears were the order of the day.

However, it was from Miss Loveday that I learnt a very important lesson which stood me in great stead years later. For some time I had been coaching a girl for Oxford, giving up endless free time, and being very anxious to get her in.

On the morning of the exam I went to wish her good luck and she turned to me and said, 'It's no use, I can't do it. I won't sit the papers, I'm too tired, and I don't know enough.'

'You must, you must,' I cried, 'think of all the work I've done with you.'

We were still arguing when the Headmistress appeared, and wanted to know what it was all about.

'Well, if she does not want to do the exam she need not,' she said, adding, 'we'll just go for a walk in the garden instead.'

I was furious and almost in tears myself but when they came back the girl had quietened down, did her exam without further fuss, and got into Oxford.

By this time I was in charge of the History department as the second teacher had gone to get married. Gradually more work was loaded on me and she was not replaced.

But the highlight of the school year was, of course, Ascot Week as the racecourse was just opposite. The senior girls, in their red cloaks were taken down to the entrance of the course to curtsey to the Royal Party as they exchanged their cars for the royal carriage. This was always a triumph for the school especially if the Queen spoke to them. But the Head was not pleased when *The Times* reported that: 'On the Queen's arrival, the Royal Berkshire Orphanage were there in their red cloaks to greet her . . .'

There was, of course, a technique for getting to the races. The Head went, wearing a large hat with a feather and sat in the Royal Enclosure. As soon as she was safely in I gave the girls an essay and together with the rest of the young Staff crossed the road. After several races we saw the feather start for home, and hastily went first. The girls were pleased to see us and said brightly, 'Had a good time, Miss Oakeley?'

But after one and a half years and with war imminent the tension in the Staff room increased.

'Do you know, Oakeley,' said the French mademoiselle, 'that Fraulein goes long walks looking for aerodromes for General Goering to bomb? You must not take her in your car near London or she will see all the big ones.'

Parents were talking about sending their girls to Canada or the States if war broke out, and some questioned having girls at school at all.

Meanwhile I was getting tired of St George's and was thinking of being called up or taking some other job. The library had been added to my work and when a big firm from London was evacuated to Ascot, I was sent to give them lectures to while away the evenings.

But I need not have worried about the future as it was already decided for me.

Chapter 6

The Outbreak of War

During the summer holidays my Father and I went on a cruise of the Western Islands of Scotland. Apart from dozens of mosquitoes and a young man who kept pestering me, it was a very happy time, the last holiday with my Father who was becoming increasingly infirm.

When we got back to Edinburgh I looked out of the hotel window and saw the news-boys in the driving rain with placards saying, 'Germans invade Poland'.

'This is it,' said my Father.

On returning home I had planned to take the Eynsham Brownies for a Pack Holiday to Swanage, but obviously it would be better to cancel it. I had started the Pack in the interval between school and Oxford and kept in touch ever since, managing three other Pack Holidays.

But I had planned without the Parents. 'Surely you are not going to let the children down, Brown Owl,' they argued. 'After all we planned our own holiday and we've paid ten shillings for theirs.' So off we went.

We had our week at Swanage, looking out each night to see if the lights had gone out, in which case it was war.

But on the Friday before war was declared I lost my nerve and phoned the buses to come and fetch us all the next day. In case of trouble on the way back I took the 'only children' in my own car, and we all arrived back tired but safe – full of virtue at having completed the journey without incident, and all well and happy.

The reception in the Square at Eynsham however was decidedly chilly.

'Poor little things cutting short their holiday by a day.' 'Shall we get some of our money back'? etc.

Even the fact that their children were clasping presents for them did not placate them.

On the Sunday, war did break out. Instead of going to church we listened to Neville Chamberlain's declaration. The following day most of the people in the village went to Oxford to stock up their larders, and I was almost alone when two buses full of pregnant Mothers arrived from

London, the Mothers having spent the night on the floor of the Corn Exchange in Witney.

Since there were none of the official Evacuation Committee in the village, my sister-in-law-to-be and I had to cope, rushing one woman off to hospital before her baby arrived. Unfortunately, hearing one of the Oxford colleges had been turned into a maternity home, I rushed her to Keble where an outraged porter assured me it was a men's college, and directed me to Ruskin.

We got them all into the local Primary School; made endless cups of tea; and sent all available children to round up the prospective hostesses saying, 'I know you asked for a nice clean little girl of eight or so, but could you take this pregnant lady and her dear little toddler instead?'

Nearly all the children had been sewn into their clothes for the winter and their heads were full of lice. Their parents had been rounded up by the police when the first Air Raid Warning went off in London; and most were dirty, too, and weeping with tiredness.

One of the most tiresome to accommodate was a lady nicknamed the Old Boozer. She had two very dirty toddlers, and was eventually put in an empty cottage by herself. Most of her time was spent in the pubs, but eventually her husband wrote to say he had found a girl 'to do for him' and she fortunately decided to go home. I was deputed to put her on the coach and she nearly missed it. For, as the coach came, saying 'Oh, luv I must just 'ave one'; she dashed into the pub and I had to rush in to prise her out.

However, the proper committee returned and I went back to St George's wondering what to do next. The first day back presented new problems as several girls had arrived from schools on the south coast, and one of them, fearing her Mother, who was still there was in danger, ran off. I was deputed to find her but after scouring the Ascot and Windsor area, decided she had gone home, which she had.

Because St George's was near all the military camps we started getting alarms, and one night, to everyone's delight we all went down into the shelters. There had long been rumours of all the delicious food stored down there, and when the Head said, 'Now girls, we are all going to have a midnight feast', everyone got excited as the cupboards were opened. But alas, they proved to be empty as the girls had raided them long ago!

Although it was at first only the phoney war, it was all very unsettling. The geography mistress was the first to go into the forces and I was told to take over her subject as well as my own; and with the job of classifying the library, I suddenly had more than enough to do. I was very glad when half term came and I had three days at home, even if it meant a drive with only small slits in my darkened headlights.

The only suggestion as to what to do next had come in a cable received three weeks before. While I had been at St James's, one of my fellow Staff had left to become Head of a New Zealand School. I had been very surprised when a cable arrived asking me if I would go out to be her senior mistress, and hastily replied in the negative. I had no wish to go to the other side of the world, and work with someone with whom I had found it hard to get on.

However, on arriving home there was another cable, and my Mother greeted me with the fact there was a second one waiting as well.

Somewhat amused I opened the first and to my astonishment read, 'Will you come to New Zealand and take my place as Head of this school?'

While I was recovering from the shock of this, I opened the second one and read, 'Earnestly desire you accept position as Head of our Church School in Timaru for which the present Head considers you most suitable. Campbell West Watson, Bishop of Christchurch.'

It was too much. Me, aged twenty-six, with four years experience – a Headmistress! I collapsed on the sofa in fits of laughter.

At this moment my Father came in. 'What on earth are you laughing at?' he demanded.

'I think they are all mad in New Zealand,' I said. 'You remember that first mad cable asking me to go to New Zealand as first assistant, and now there have been two more. One asking me to be Headmistress by the present Head, and another asking the same thing from a Bishop.'

I handed him the cables and he studied them carefully. 'I'm not sure you are not being rather foolish,' he said. 'It is not everyone who is offered a headship at twenty-six. At your age you have nothing to lose and you can always come home at the end of your contract with nothing to lose, and without harming your career. The only alternative is to go into the services and I know you are not keen on that. I think you should consider it.'

I was completely taken aback, and I did start thinking about it. It all seemed so far away, a country of which I knew nothing and so far removed from my family and friends. On the other hand I was tired of teaching at St George's so I cabled for more information and was told to see the school's agent in London.

This turned out to be an organisation called the Church Teachers's Organisation and I duly went up to London and found the offices at the bottom of Whitehall. They had the smallest imaginable office, presided over by an elderly lady with a large bun.

'Whatever made them offer this job to you?' she said crossly. 'The school has had enough troubles without this. Three Heads in three years and now the new one meeting a widower with five children on the boat, and marrying him. You look far too young for the job, my dear.'

'I'm twenty-six.' I said defiantly, 'twenty-seven in April.'

The elderly lady shuffled her papers.

'I cannot stop you, unless you refuse to go,' she replied. 'The school has sent a contract for you to sign, so we must do it, but I shall certainly make it clear to the Bishop that I do not approve of your appointment.'

So the contract was produced, and we duly signed it, and I knew I had burnt my boats.

The said Mary Oakeley of The Gables, Eynsham, Oxon, England to be Headmistress of Craighead Diocesan School, Timaru, New Zealand for four years, starting February 1940; to have the right to appoint her own staff; and in all things to be controlled by the Bishop and Standing Committee of the Diocese of Christchurch, New Zealand. Her passage to be paid one way, and the salary to be £400 a year plus board and lodging.

I read it through once more. I had looked up Timaru in the atlas and found it on the eastern side of the South Island between Christchurch and Dunedin. The good lady had no idea how many girls there were, how many members of Staff existed and if the school was in a town or right out in the country.

As I wrote my name I knew I had made an irrevocable step, and wondered what the outcome would be. To go to the other side of the world in wartime, to a land where I knew no one; a land peopled by Maoris, kiwis and the godly descendants of the early settlers of the 1840s seemed an adventure indeed.

But now there was to be no turning back. The signing finished, I turned to go, but the good lady put up a restraining hand.

'My dear,' she said kindly, 'I cannot stop this most unfortunate decision, but there is one thing we can do.' With that she cleared a space among the papers on the floor, and knelt down in prayer. I followed suit and for five minutes she prayed long and earnestly that some way would be found out of this awful dilemma, and God would direct me (perhaps to change my mind) and the future of this famous school would be assured in the best possible way.

By the end of it, I was nearly in tears, and I left the office very depressed. I wept most of the way back in the train, and on and off. I started packing my belongings. I bought a large cabin trunk with my initials on it, and in it packed my precious books, my scanty wardrobe, and a few personal possessions.

Hurriedly I took my MA paying the statutory £15 and bought a second-hand gown and crimson hood from the widow of a man killed in a road accident. I thought it would look more dignified than my rather tatty white bunny fur, and I was going to need all the dignity I could muster. Money was short and clothes already hard to get but I took my Mother's advice for which I was ever grateful and bought a really smart outfit for my arrival.

Then it was back to St George's at almost the end of term to give in my notice. Like everyone else they were astonished and kindly gave me many presents and wished me luck. How I wished I knew a little more about how schools were run, how one managed Staff and even how one made a timetable.

All too soon came the time to leave. With a sinking heart I left my home, saying goodbye to the maids, the gardeners, the Dandie Dinmonts and above all my seventy-year-old father whom I should probably not see again. The phoney war was in progress and apart from the sinking of the *Graf Spee*, nothing much seemed to have happened. I tried to cheer myself with the thought that the war would not last long, and I could get home if I could not manage the job.

My Mother had decided to come down to Southampton with me but up to the last minute I was not sure if the arrangement was on or off. The period between Christmas and February is a holiday in New Zealand and it was only a few days before I sailed that the passage money arrived. It was bitterly cold everywhere and when we arrived in Southampton there was no heating in the hotel and the food was terrible. I could not wait to join the *Orontes* which was the ship in which I was to sail as the agony of those last days with my Mother was almost more than I could bear. Years later I saw her diary: 'Said Goodbye to my dear Mary, one of the saddest days of my life'.

Next day, with both of us in tears, I said my last goodbye and suitcase in hand went on board the *Orontes*, lying with snow covered decks in Southampton docks. The first thing seemed to be to find the Purser's office and discover where my cabin was situated.

On finding it I had a nasty shock.

'Didn't you get the message?' asked the Purser. 'We struck one of those new magnetic mines in the Thames just after we had left London. It has not done a great deal of damage but the sailing will be delayed about a week. The London Office was asked to inform all passengers, and ask them to delay their arrival by one week.'

My heart sank. The thought of going home after all those farewells, perhaps even rejoining my Mother if she had not left Southampton appalled me. But I need not have worried because the Purser was speaking again.

'I am afraid you will have to stay now,' he said. 'Once passengers have embarked and seen the position of the guns they cannot go ashore again. I am afraid it will not be very comfortable while the ship is in dock but perhaps you can make the best of it.'

So carrying my things I went dejectedly to Cabin 143 on D Deck and was relieved to find that at least the school had paid for a single cabin, small as it was, and a friendly steward arrived to unpack my things.

So a dreary week passed as a solitary passenger. All the officers were too busy to entertain me and I crouched over a one-bar heater in the passenger lounge trying to get warm. My one consolation was that I had with me the twelve volumes of the books by Mazo de la Roche which I had always loved and I sat down to read them.

At last the damage was repaired and I brightened up as I stood on deck and watched the other passengers arriving. Most of them were Australians and New Zealanders, loaded with luggage, returning home from the cold and the war, and glad to get away before things got worse.

I found myself at a table with an elderly Australian lady who told me it was going to be a very dangerous voyage and she doubted if we would survive it. She intended to sleep in her clothes until she got home to Melbourne in case we were torpedoed. Feeling I could not face this for six weeks I moved to the fourth officer's table which was more amusing.

After the evening meal we all went up to see the ship sail. A howling blizzard was raging and Southampton docks were deep in snow. There were no farewells, no one to cheer us on our way as the time of departure had to be kept secret. As we passed the Isle of Wight we saw several destroyers and cruisers and a convoy lining up for the Middle East. Overhead, seagulls moaned and I thought of my parents sitting by the fire listening to the evening news; of my little dog Jillie, looking for me to give her her evening meal; and of lots of little girls in a foreign country wondering what their new Headmistress would be like.

An even denser blizzard blotted out the land as we sped down the

48

Channel. There were no more ships and the outline of England faded out and there was a sense of dense blackness and a feeling of desolation and separation.

CRAIGHEAD

Chapter 7

The Voyage

Next morning I woke to a very rough sea. The porthole was permanently closed because of the black-out and being a very bad sailor I dressed hurriedly and staggered out to get some fresh air. It had ceased snowing but was bitterly cold and I soon retired to the lounge and Mazo de la Roche.

However, we were soon disturbed by people staggering up for boat drill, and to hear instructions on how to make a Panic Bag in case we were torpedoed. It included a packet of anti-shark powder in case we sank in the Indian Ocean! The ship seemed to be travelling at a great rate and it was explained to me that the big ships had refused to go in convoy because it meant going slow and so increasing the risk of being sunk. The captains of the smaller ships often exaggerated the speed at which they could go and in consequence the whole convoy was slowed down and became a sitting target. We were, therefore, making a dash for Gibraltar on our own.

In spite of this we ran into trouble next day. I was sound asleep at 7am when the steward opened the door and shouted, 'Wake up, Miss! Enemy submarine sighted. Ship's going into action. All passengers to go to the dining-room.'

I tumbled out of bed, seized my Panic Bag, put on a dressing gown and joined a line of frightened people all hurrying to the dining-room. There we sat at our tables while the ship zig-zagged at top speed, and we tried to reassure ourselves and each other by saying how slow the new U-boats were, and anyway no enemy would sink a passenger ship full of women and children – or so we hoped. Some of the passengers were crying, one was reading her Bible out loud, but most of us were trying to be very brave and British.

After half an hour the ship steadied, the stewards told us we had outdistanced the submarine, and we retired to our cabins to get dressed.

Three days later some wag opened my cabin door at 8am and shouted, 'The ship's going into action'. Once more seizing my Panic Bag, and not waiting to take the curlers out of my hair, I rushed into the dining-room only to find it was a practical joke and everyone was peacefully eating their breakfast. Like Queen Victoria 'I was not amused'.

All the same we did not feel very safe, especially as we were the last ship to go through the Mediterranean before Italy entered the war. As we passed Cape Trafalgar we saw a small freighter on its way north. Later we heard it had been sunk by the same U-boat which had chased us.

After we had passed Gibraltar we felt safer as we heard that Italy still had not come into the war. The harbour was full of ships, two French destroyers, three British sloops and a mass of others. It was all rather disappointing as we were not allowed to land for security reasons, but we were cheered by hearing we would be allowed to land at Naples.

On 26 January we entered the beautiful Bay of Naples. It was a fine sunny morning and we made up a party to go to see Pompeii. It included two young civil servants who were going out to Saudi Arabia, and who wanted to have a last fling before they went to work. They were particularly doleful when we had a slight shower of rain, and said it could be the last they would see for many years.

However, we had a very interesting day at Pompeii, and arrived back with large bouquets of flowers. Then on to Port Said where we said goodbye to the two young men, and on through the Suez Canal and the Red Sea which was just as hot as we had always been told. However, Aden was even hotter but by now all danger was over and we could enjoy ourselves.

The port of call I most wanted to see was Colombo and I made plans to go up to Kandy to see Buddha's tooth, and the marvellous temple about which I had heard so much. However, it was not to be! The day before we got there I developed German measles, much to my disgust. I was immediately moved to a stateroom on A Deck and everyone was most sympathetic. The Captain and officers sent me flowers and I came to the conclusion I was the most popular girl in the ship.

Little did I know the reason for this solicitude! When we had called at Naples there was a New Zealand boy waiting to join the ship but he had very unfortunately developed German measles. Under the regulations the Captain was not allowed to take infectious cases on board, but if the boy was left he would probably be interned as Italy was about to come into the war, although actually it was some months before she did come in. Since we were the last passenger ship to call at Naples, it was finally decided to take him on board and he was smuggled into the hospital. As I had played deck tennis with the doctor and nurse it was concluded I must have caught German measles through them and I might sue the Company for damages! Hence all the solicitude!

Nothing was further from my mind. I was wholly taken up with self pity at missing Colombo and very relieved when the week was over and I could return to my own small cabin. All the same it was very embarrassing when the next batch came out with German measles. It included the Purser, two stokers, three members of the deck crew and several officers, and by the time we got to Melbourne half the ship was down with it and we were flying the yellow flag.

It was in Melbourne I got my first letter from my Mother. After the usual enquiries and home news she concluded: 'I hope you are all right, dear. We have been worried that the children, with whom you went to tea just before you left have all had German measles.'

And so we came to Australia, and berthed at Fremantle, blinking our eyes at the lights burning all night; at barrowfuls of grapes at fantastically low prices; and the first sight of a land so like, and yet unlike, the one we had left. We drove up into Perth, surely one of the most beautiful cities in the world, situated on the Swan River and with some of the best laid-out gardens in King's Park. Then on to Adelaide with its superb view from Mount Lofty, and so to Melbourne where friends met me and took me to see the Melbourne Cup which was won by the famous Australian horse Ajax. The day was somewhat marred by struggling to eat twelve raw oysters for lunch!

However, all voyages, however pleasant come to an end and on 26 February we were up at dawn to pass through the heads into the beautiful harbour of Sydney. It was a perfect sunny morning and the sea was an aquamarine blue. Sydney was living up to its claim to have the most beautiful harbour in the world and soon we saw the great bridge which now dominates it. The docks were crowded with Australians welcoming home their relatives and we said goodbye to many of our friends. The *Orontes* went no further but would load with wool and apples and return to Britain where it later became a troop ship.

I could not help being rather forlorn as I collected my hand luggage and prepared for the four-day voyage to New Zealand. It seems incredible to think of how short a time the journey now takes by air!

I went down to the Purser's office to find out where I got the boat for New Zealand and was told it left from one of the further quays in half an hour.

I was bitterly disappointed as I had looked forward to seeing Sydney and had imagined I would have at least two days there. My Australian friends on the boat had told me about all the wonderful things to see, and I knew Sydney was one of the most beautiful and gayest cities in the world.

Fortunately I had already delayed and by not hurrying conveniently missed the New Zealand boat. I was, however, in a quandary as we were only allowed to bring £10 from England and that had already been spent. I knew no one in Sydney with whom I could stay; and when I made further inquiries I found the next boat was the *Mariposa* which was not sailing for another week. There was nothing for it but to go to the Purser and to tell him how stupid I had been. He was duly sympathetic and allowed me to stay in the ship while it was loading which solved all my problems.

And what a week it was! I was the only passenger left in the ship. Some of the officers and the nursing sister were free at odd times and we went surfing at Manly and Bondi; we danced and ate lobsters at Princes; we visited lovely Vaucluse; and went to Tauronga Park to play with the koalas. On top of this there were endless parties with the Australians who had sailed with us.

Friday 1 March saw the end of the idyll. It was raining hard as I left the *Orontes* and all my friends and drove up to the *Mariposa* which was an American ship going to Auckland. It differed in many ways from the *Orontes*. My cabin had no porthole and was very hot and we had enormous platefuls at every meal, most of which people left. Coming from wartime England where food was already very short, I felt embarrassed by the waste.

The *Mariposa* was full of New Zealanders going home, and for the first time I got news of my school.

'You're not going to Craighead are you? Why, it's due to close any time.'

'All the best schools are in the North Island. Most South Island girls travel north to them.'

'Of course, Craighead was once a good school. It was founded by the Misses Shand, and as long as they were there it was well known. The next Head, Miss Salmond who came out from England, was given the wrong anaesthetic in the Christchurch Hospital, when she was having her tonsils out, and died suddenly.'

'You don't mean you are going to be Headmistress of Craighead? They must be out of their minds to appoint someone so young and inexperienced after all their troubles.' Someone even said they had three if not four Headmistresses in three years.

All this was very depressing. Having little idea of what life was like in New Zealand, I was taken by an elderly gentleman who told me it was essential for me to learn Maori and we sat down on deck with a Maori grammar while I repeated slowly 'Wai-kar-i-mo-ana' and 'Pae-kak-ar-iki'. Needless to say that apart from finding out that the Maoris give equal stress to each syllable, I was none the wiser.

Among the passengers was the New Zealand opera singer, Oscar Natske who had left New Zealand as a young man after working in a blacksmith's shop and within three years was singing at Covent Garden, and become famous. It was five years since he had left New Zealand and now he was famous and reporters were waiting for him in Auckland. He was due to sing in the New Zealand Centennial Programme and would later return to finish his studies at Covent Garden. I was much amused when I asked if he would sing something for me.

He replied haughtily, 'It would cost you £50 for me to open my mouth.'

The four days at sea seemed endless. There had been no word from the school since I left and all these depressing stories made me very apprehensive. Was it all a great mistake? Would the school be closed when I got there? What should I do if it was? I was hardly qualified for any other job.

Then at last I met someone who gave me hope. It was the last night before we landed in Auckland and everyone, except me, was feeling in a happy mood. The New Zealanders were craning their necks for a view of the land which Abel Tasman had described as 'a great land uplifted high', and were busy telling us it was the best country in the world with no class distinctions or distracting wars, and there was plenty to eat and drink. As I sat listening and wondering how I should get on in a land where I knew no one and in a school with so many difficulties, an elderly woman came up and sat next to me.

'I hear you are going to be Headmistress of Craighead School in Timaru,' she volunteered.

'Yes,' I replied rather despondently. 'I hear on all sides it is in a bad way, practically closing down some people say. I am wondering what will happen to me if it does.'

She picked up her knitting. 'Now don't you worry,' she said. 'Maybe it is in a bad way. I was there myself in the days of the Misses Shands. It was a good school then and it can become one again if it has the right Head.'

'But I'm so young,' I moaned, reiterating what so many people had said to me.

'Good on you,' she answered. 'Why, that's just what they want! Someone young and energetic who can put new life into the place. I suppose you have a fixed contract and unless you get married you'll be there at least four years and that will give them some continuity.'

'Do you really think I've got a chance?' I hazarded.

'Of course you have. They have a strong Old Girls Association and they will back you even if they think this is the last chance the school will get. It's true there are well established and beautiful schools in the North Island but people don't all want to send their daughters across the straits unless they have to. Most of the old Canterbury families supported Craighead in the past and will do so again if they get a decent Headmistress with high ideals, energy and ability.'

I thanked her heartily. This was the first encouragement I had had and my spirits rose. I joined Oscar Natske on the rails of the ship.

'This is a great day for me,' he said. 'I left New Zealand a poor boy from a forge in Auckland. I return a world famous singer invited by the New Zealand Government to sing at the Centennial.'

'This is a great day for me, too,' I said. 'I come to New Zealand to a country where I know no one, to work among people I have never met, and like you I am aiming at success and the start of a new life.'

Next morning we docked at Auckland. The quay was full of noisy New Zealanders welcoming their friends and relations home, with their arms full of flowers and streamers. They were whiling away the time while we waited to land by singing Maori songs. Outside the rain was falling steadily.

I stood on the deck of the *Mariposa* looking at the scene. This was to be my home for four years; these people were to be my fellow workers and friends; and this country, looking dreary in the falling rain, was to be my host and my destiny.

There was no one to meet me, no word of welcome. Picking up my hand luggage, sticking my chin out firmly and holding my head high, I walked down the gangway into a new world.

Chapter 8

Arrival

I sat on my luggage in the Auckland Customs, wondering how I was going to spend the day. I had found out the train to Wellington did not leave until early evening. I was appalled at the idea of wandering about in a strange city in a strange country.

Suddenly I saw a bright, attractive New Zealand girl bearing down on me. 'Are you Mary Oakeley?' she asked. 'Some friends of yours in England wrote to me, and asked me to meet you, and I saw in the paper you were arriving today. I've come to take you out to our beach by the sea for the day, and then I'll put you on the train for Wellington this evening.'

I have never forgotten the kindness of her and her husband and the happy day I spent with them in Auckland. Without them it would have been a miserable day and in after years when I had overseas staff arriving in Auckland, I always made sure there was someone to meet them and look after them for the day.

After a very pleasant day when I learnt a lot about life in New Zealand, I caught the bus to the station and boarded the train for Wellington. This still remains the worst journey I have ever experienced by train!

The train was called the Limited and I could only get a seat with my back to the engine, opposite a Japanese gentleman who was sick into a paper bag at intervals as the train groaned and swayed over the New Zealand mountains. There were endless stops when everyone seemed to get out for five to ten minutes. I was afraid to do so as I feared I might be left behind, and anyway I imagined they were all greeting their friends and relations. I waited and waited for the call to dinner in the restaurant but it never came. It was only next morning after a sleepless night that I realised if you wanted anything to eat on New Zealand trains you had to jump out and get it. On top of everything the train was very overcrowded because the victorious sailors from the *Achilles* which had helped sink the *Graf Spee* were on board, and naturally spent the night celebrating.

And so, hungry, tired and dirty I arrived in Wellington three hours late. There was still no word from the school, so I wandered about visiting the Centennial Exhibition, and admiring the British Pavilion. I also visited a few shops and had my hair done.

In the evening I joined the South Island Ferry and there at last was a telegram from the school. It said, 'Greetings from Craighead Old Girls,' and was signed Dorothy Raymond. At last someone was expecting me I thought.

An hour later another telegram arrived. 'Will meet you under clock Christchurch Station tomorrow. Theo West Watson.'

I puzzled over this. Was it the Bishop's wife or his daughter? I should soon see but it was another bad night, sharing a cabin with a mother and baby, and the latter cried for most of it.

However, next morning I dressed very carefully, put on my best hat, but unfortunately could not find my gloves which seemed to be lost. It was explained to me that to get to Christchurch you had to take a train from the port of Lytellton where the ferry docked and go through a tunnel under the hills, to the city. The early settlers had to struggle over the hills, dragging their wardrobes and grand pianos with them! So I got in the train, went through the tunnel and arrived on Christchurch station.

I walked towards the clock. The only person there was an attractive elderly lady in grey, correct in hat and gloves. She looked at me for some time and then said, 'You're not Miss Oakeley, I hope?'

'Yes, I am,' I replied.

She looked me up and down. 'I am the Bishop's sister, and he asked me to meet you. I am afraid he is expecting a much older woman. How old are you?' she asked.

Timidly I replied, 'Twenty-seven.'

She looked appalled. 'The Bishop thinks you are thirty-seven, and I am afraid he will be very upset.' Then she added, 'and where are your gloves?'

'I'm afraid I've lost them,' I quavered.

'Then we had better go and buy some before we go to Bishops' Court,' she replied.

We got into Miss West Watson's little car, and drove off. We bought some gloves and then went to Bishops' Court, a beautiful house, where Campbell West Watson, once the Boy Bishop of Barrow in Furness, and now Bishop of Christchurch lived with his sister and younger son. His wife had died some years before and was much missed in Christchurch where she had been much loved.

We got out at Bishops' Court front door, and I was left in the hall wearing my new gloves, and clutching my small suitcase, while Miss

West Watson went to break it to the Bishop that yet another disaster had befallen the unfortunate Craighead, in that the new Headmistress was not only too young but quite unsuitable.

After a few minutes the Bishop appeared.

'My dear Miss Oakeley,' he said, 'welcome to Christchurch and to New Zealand, but my sister tells me there has be some mistake about your age. Is it true you are only twenty-seven? If so you would be younger than any of your Staff and your predecessor who recommended you said you were thirty-seven.'

'Yes, my Lord, it is true,' I replied, 'but I shall be twenty-eight in a few months' time,' I added hopefully.

'Well,' he said kindly,' you must have breakfast, and then you shall have a rest as you look very tired. In the meanwhile I will gather together the members of the Standing Committee of Synod to see what we can do about this most difficult situation.'

So we had breakfast, and I was taken up to my room, where on opening my suitcase I found all my family photos broken, and I had a little weep, since there was no one in this strange country on whose shoulders I could cry my heart out.

After a rest I felt better, and in the afternoon, the Headmistress of the Christchurch Diocesan School arrived to interview me. I seemed horribly inexperienced and when she talked about Standard Six I thought she meant Form Six and thought they must be very backward in New Zealand!

Meanwhile the Standing Committee was meeting in the drawing-room and after tea I was sent for to meet them. The Bishop was presiding and he kindly asked me to sit down, which I did.

'Now Miss Oakeley,' he began, 'there has obviously been a terrible mistake. If we had known how young you were we should obviously not have appointed you as Head of our Timaru School. Craighead has had many disasters in the last few years and it needs someone experienced and mature. We are all very sorry there has been this mistake but you will appreciate that it would be most unsuitable for you to take over a school where most of the staff are older than you are. Indeed we have contacted the school and the Archdeacon feels as we do that you are far too young for the post.'

There was a pause.

Then he went on. 'So, we have been in contact with a retired Headmistress in the North Island, and she is willing to take on the school for a few years, and then perhaps you will be ready for a Headship. After working under her as her First Assistant you will be more experienced and accustomed to New Zealand ways.'

There was a dead silence. Everyone was looking at me. I stood facing them, utterly alone, like Luther at the Diet of Worms with a pile of faggots waiting outside. I felt very young, alone and unhappy. Was this really timid little me facing this horrible situation?

Hesitatingly I began, 'I'm sorry, my Lord Bishop, and members of the Standing Committee, but you engaged me as Headmistress and not as a First Assistant. Your agent saw me in London and signed my contract. (I was glad my Father had insisted I had one.) I may be young and inexperienced but I could not come to a strange country and work under someone I have not seen and do not know. I am quite willing to go back to England if you will pay my passage but if I stay it will be as Headmistress. This was the post for which you engaged me and I would not consider any other. If I stay I would of course do my best to improve the school.'

Amazed at my temerity I sat down. They all looked astounded. I was dismissed and discussions began again. An hour later I was called back and Judge Gresson, the Chairman, spoke.

'Well, Miss Oakeley,' he said, 'as you insist we have no choice but to let you try the post for one year. We are naturally most apprehensive about the whole situation, but our prayers and good wishes go with you, in the taking up of a most difficult task.'

Later I knew they had not the money to pay my passage back, but then I tried to thank them and at that moment tea came in and we had a rather stultified meal with everyone trying to be nice to me. I felt like a lamb going to the slaughter.

Meanwhile the Bishop telephoned the school and told them what had happened. I heard the Bishops' sister say, 'What *did* they say, Campbell?'

'They are very upset,' he answered, 'and do not see how it can possibly work.'

That evening the Bishop and his sister did all they could to be nice to me, and the kind old man said he would drive me down to Timaru the next day, so that it would soften the blow. I gathered the Archdeacon was furious and would prefer the school closed.

I spent a restless night, but the next day was sunny and I packed my case and got ready for the Big Adventure.

'I don't care what anyone thinks,' I said to myself. 'I'm going to show them all that their rundown school can be put on its feet. They have no money to send me home, so they've got to have me, and must make the best of it. I'll make a success of it somehow.'

Before we left the kindly Bishop took me to his Chapel and after praying with him, I felt calmer and more able to face the ordeal to come. Miss West Watson came to see me off.

'You must make this your home,' she said kindly, 'and do not hesitate to ring if you want any advice.' She paused and then said, 'But oh, my dear, you look so terribly young in that hat! It will never do. I'll get you one of mine.'

She went hurriedly into Bishops' Court and reappeared with a large hat with a sheaf of flowers in front, like the ones my Mother used to wear. My heart sank. It was bad enough going to this strange and hostile school where no one wanted me, but to wear someone else's hat was the end! Gingerly I tried it on and was much relieved my head was so large.

'It's very kind of you,' I said with relief, 'but it won't go on.' And off it came and back went my own C and A creation, sitting on the top of my head.

And so we said goodbye to Bishops' Court, and in years to come I never forgot all the kindness I received from the Bishop and his sister, who always welcomed me in the holidays and helped me in a thousand ways.

The Bishop drove me down slowly the hundred miles to Timaru, pointing out little things on the way.

As we passed Riccarton, he pointed out the little English church. 'In this little country churchyard which reminds me of England,' he said, 'my wife is buried there – and I shall lie beside her,' he added. Years later when I went back to visit New Zealand I stood beside his grave and thanked God for a very wonderful and kind man.

Halfway there we stopped in Ashburton, and called on the Archdeacon and his wife. She took me aside into the kitchen. 'You must not go racing,' she said. 'Your predecessor did and it is not right for the Headmistress of a Church school to go betting.'

I did not feel this would be a great temptation, so I just said I would be careful. Obviously there were going to be a lot of things it was not seemly for a Headmistress to do!

So we drove on, across the Canterbury Plains, with the beautiful mountains on the right, and the sea away on the left. At last we saw a sign which said, 'Timaru' and my heart beat faster, and I felt sick with fright.

We turned away from the sea, and went up Wai iti Road and into Sealy Street. At the end I saw a large white building, sadly lacking paint.

'This is your school,' said the Bishop, 'and may God bless it and all your work in it.'

Chapter 9

First Impressions

We went up a tree-lined drive, and halted in front of the main entrance. The reception committee was waiting. It was headed by the Archdeacon who had opposed my appointment, even before he knew my age. He had given up all hope of the school ever flourishing, and wanted it to close. The only two who were not looking glum were the President of the Old Girls Association, Dorothy Raymond, who smiled a welcome, and the school secretary, Mr Bryan King.

I had been very surprised that the school had a male secretary, and there had been many jokes on the ship as to what he would be like. No one had forecast a staid elderly gentleman, who looked like a Dickens character but I was to find him a tower of strength in those difficult early days.

I was duly introduced to all the Governors and tried to chat cheerfully. The five members of Staff, headed by an elderly and rather formidable Matron were also introduced but there were no girls about, though I suspected a few eyes were peeping out of the windows.

'Well, Miss Oakeley,' said the Bishop breaking an awkward silence, 'you had better enter your school,' and he gave a little bow as we entered. So up the steps we went, and into a gloomy hall, notable for its dark brown paint.

'Matron will show you round,' said the Bishop, and round we went. Three dormitories were shut up for lack of girls; holes in the linoleum everywhere; walls with the paint peeling off; and a Headmistress' sitting-room at the back, so dark the light was always on. The kitchen was indescribable, like something out of Hogarth. But there were some good points. The Old Girls had recently given a splendid swimming pool; there was a large and spacious gymnasium; and I had a small and lovely bedroom looking across towards the mountains or hills as the New Zealanders called them. I could see Four Peaks and Mount Peel, and later when I got depressed at the enormity of the task before me, I could lift up my eyes unto the hills whence cometh help.

After lunch in a small and gloomy dining-room, the parents and Old Girls were assembled in the gym. I was glad my Mother had made me buy a smart new outfit. I had never spoken in public to a large assembly before, but I did my best, saying how pleased I was to have come to the school, which I thought was beautiful, and which had great possibilities.

'You could not have meant what you said,' remarked someone afterwards. 'This school has had it, to put it bluntly.'

'Well,' I replied, 'it has had a lot of bad luck but I am here to stay and give it stability.'

Several parents told me their daughters would be leaving to go to better schools at the end of the year, and I told them how sorry I was they would not be helping to put the school on its feet. Nevertheless I could see they were not all convinced, and I saw some hard work ahead. The school had once been of nearly 200 but now there were 43: 21 boarders and 22 day girls.

When the party was over I said goodbye to the kindly Bishop who was taking over the post of Chairman of Governors since the Archdeacon was giving up. At least I knew there was one person who would help and support me in the future.

So far I had seen little of the girls. The only one I had encountered was in one of the dormitories when Matron was showing me round. She was sitting weeping and when I inquired why, Matron told me, 'I'm afraid all the girls are disappointed as they had hoped for someone older.'

So now with all the visitors gone, I gathered the boarders together and surveyed them. At one end of the scale were Margaret and Patricia aged just five. Both of them lived in back country sheep stations, far away from any school or doctor. Margaret's brother had died of appendicitis because the river near the station was in full flood and they could not get across and anxious parents had brought her down to school. At the other end was the Head Prefect, Margot aged nineteen and I could see the problems Matron faced at bedtime, and entertainments for such a wide range of girls at the weekends. Because of the small numbers the forms contained a wide age range and one had only three girls aged 12, 13 and 15.

'What would you do to improve this school?' I asked when I had them all together. But the answers were disappointing.

'The only good schools are in the North Island. You should see the buildings at Woodford or Nga Tawa!'

'We're a dud school. We're too small to win any matches and we always get beaten. I agree with my parents. It should be closed.'

Somewhat disappointed, I said Goodnight and settled down to think.

Obviously the school had its good points. I liked the First Assistant who seemed keen and anxious to help; there was plenty of equipment but no library; and the school had a beautiful site looking towards the mountains and the sea. But it lacked grounds. The only playing field was across the road in a public park and the one tennis court was too near the school windows. In the past the school had relied on overseas teaching Staff, but these had ceased with the war, and few young New Zealanders would teach in private schools. In consequence the school relied on part-time retired teachers who, other than teaching, took little part in school life, or trained primary teachers who could not teach the Sixth Form.

I had plenty of time to think things over as I had to share a bathroom with the girls, and the last light was not out till ten. By then, of course the water was stone cold!

However the next day the sun was shining, and my first caller appeared. 'Mrs Percy Elworthy,' the Matron announced.

Mrs Elworthy had lived in England and had connections with some of my relations. What a relief it was to sit down and talk about them with someone who knew people I knew, and moreover she gave me much good advice.

'This is a good school if you can really get it going,' she said. 'You'll find people will stop sending their girls to the North Island if you can really get it going and if there is a good school here. It is going to be dangerous to cross the Straits if the Japs come into the war. But you'll have to get your buildings painted, get some good qualified staff and you'll have to stop looking so young. Parents are already thinking you won't be responsible enough, and you will have to reassure them. You must do something about your hats. They just won't do!'

Her visit meant much to me. Like all New Zealanders she was profuse in her offers of hospitality and coming from one of the most influential families in the South Island, her favourable report on me would be of great assistance. Mrs Elworthy gave me the strength I badly needed and I was greatly cheered and helped by her visit.

So the next day I went off to the local shop and asked the assistant for a new hat.

'Something to make me look old,' I pleaded.

'Most people, Madam, want a hat to make them look younger,' answered the assistant, and produced a selection of Hats for Matrons. None of them fitted and I finally abandoned the hat problem.

I did however, benefit from the rest of Mrs Elworthy's advice. Painting and teaching Staff became a top priority. That evening, the Matron, First

Headmistress of Craighead 1940–1955

Assistant and I sat down with pencil and paper and drew up a plan. First we must restore confidence in the school, and make people think it could be efficient and well run. Wherever we went, and especially at the Morning Tea Parties, where the gossip of the town was analysed, we must tell people that the school was on the upgrade. We must also make the girls proud of their school, improve its academic standards, and make some better arrangement for the very young children. Somehow we must find funds to build proper class rooms, a library and some science laboratories, which at present consisted of one room at the back of the school.

Above all something must be done about a School Chapel. A small room in the house had been set aside for one, but if the school grew it would obviously not be large enough. On Sundays the school went down to the parish church but there was no proper school service. If Craighead was to be a proper Christian Diocesan School, a chapel was essential.

Much, however, would depend on the Old Girls who seemed the only group with confidence in the school. Soon after my arrival I went to their reception, in a white hat with a bow on the top, and outlined the help I needed. They were enthusiastic and I began to feel I had at least one group behind me.

That evening there was an informal party at the house of one of the Old Girls in Geraldine, a town near Timaru. I was driven out to the beautiful home of the Burdon family. This was the true New Zealand, a beautiful home, marvellous food cooked by the hostess, and happy friendly people. To my amazement there were no Staff behind it all, only Mary in the kitchen to help wash up, but everything done perfectly for a huge party. Indeed I met so many people it was hard to take them all in.

'I hear you think Craighead is not so bad,' someone volunteered, 'but of course it would not compare with schools in England.'

I replied, 'Well, there are not many English schools with such a lovely swimming pool, and I think Craighead has great possibilities.'

'You'll never make a go of it,' growled an elderly farmer. 'You'll be gone in no time and there will be four Heads in three years instead of three, and the school will close.'

'I've got a four year contract,' I reminded him.

This was the first time I had met New Zealand drinking habits. After wartime England where drink was scarce there seemed a great abundance of gin and whisky, and I came to the conclusion I had a very poor head compared to everyone else. At this time all the pubs closed at six, and most of the drinking had to go on surreptitiously or in private houses. Moreover, women did not drink in hotels, only at home or in other private houses.

It was at this party that the disadvantages of being a Headmistress were brought home to me. After all, it did not look very suitable for a Headmistress to return after midnight on her fourth day in New Zealand and I had a long day ahead of me! The question was how to get back. The friends who had brought me obviously thought it was far too early to go home. However, an offer came from an unexpected quarter.

One of the young men at the party came up and offered to take me home on his motor bike. What fun I thought! It was a lovely moonlight night and it was not very far. As always in New Zealand it was warm and pleasant and I went off to get my coat.

As I was going one of the older ladies came up to me.

'My dear,' she said, 'you're not intending to go home on a motor bike with a young man, are you? Surely you must see it would never do for a Headmistress to be seen on such a form of transport! The whole countryside would be talking and where would your job and reputation be then? You really cannot do it.'

I saw the point. From now on I must behave like a middle-aged schoolmarm if I wanted my school to flourish, and keep away from such things as motor bikes and such people as young men. Reluctantly I found the owner of the bike and said on second thoughts that it was too cold, and I was a little frightened of riding pillion. He was rather disappointed but seemed to understand.

My hostess saw what had happened and hastily found an elderly farmer and his wife with a nice big car, and persuaded them to take me home. I now knew more forcibly that it was very difficult to be both young and a Headmistress.

Chapter 10

Starting to work

One of the first things I had to do after my arrival was to apologise to a Miss Walton. Apparently she was a very influential lady, whose father was Deputy Chairman of the Governors and she was kind enough to take the Gardening Class at the school. On the day of my arrival the gardeners had all downed tools and departed to the shrubbery to get a look at their new Headmistress, and she was left to put everything away!

Feeling rather cross at having to apologise for something I had not done, I went to call at Miss Walton's home, only to find Dorothy Walton was the same age as me, was not affected by the incident at all, and we soon became friends.

It was she who saved me at Easter Week which fell soon after my arrival. It had never occurred to anyone that if all the teaching and domestic Staff, and the boarders went off for their Easter Exeat, I should be left entirely alone. As I was no cook the prospect of a week alone in the school building was bleak indeed.

I was sitting alone on the school steps in front of the main building, trying to fight off homesickness, and keep the tears from my eyes when Dorothy Walton came to look for some lost gardening tools and hearing of my plight invited me to her cottage at Peel Forest for the Exeat. Here for the first time I saw the lovely New Zealand Bush and woke to the sound of the bell birds. The friendship with the Walton family was to stand me in good stead in my plans for the school, but like everything else it had its problems, including a visit from one of the Old Girls objecting to my allowing Dorothy to call me by my Christian name!

Easter over, I got down to make plans for the school. First I looked up all the Staff dossiers, and read their testimonials. Then I visited each class in turn, talked to them and listened to the lessons. I was relieved to find the five teachers I had were all good and anxious to teach well, even if they were lacking in experience. I found I had to teach full time myself, and administration had to be done at night when school had finished.

Then I looked at the list of entries, and found that in the last two years there had been only one new girl.

'It is a waste of time expecting people to send their girls here,' said my First Assistant, 'even those whose names are down are not expecting to come.'

'I'll jolly well make them,' I replied hopefully.

So I sat down and wrote in longhand to everyone who had ever thought of sending their daughter to the school. I had by now discovered that Mr Bryan King was only secretary to the Governors, and I had no secretarial assistance whatever.

To every prospective parent I wrote in the same vein. That I had come out from England for four years; that I found much to praise in the school; and I was looking forward to their daughter joining it. I got some very indignant letters back! How did I ever think they would send their daughter to Craighead. She was already booked for one of the *efficient* schools in the North Island. Some, however, did write nice letters and suggested coming to see me.

Then I badgered people for a list of girls of school age anywhere in the South Island, and wrote to their parents saying if they had not already chosen a school, would they come and look at Craighead before they decided? Some nights I was writing letters till well after midnight and the Secretary complained about the high cost of postage!

A week later my first prospective parents arrived. I was in a great state. Suppose I failed to enrol their daughter! It did not bear thinking about. I put on my best dress and waited.

Fortunately they were charming people. I did my best but could not remember where the awful science laboratory was situated. I ought to have known it was the worst room in the school – at the back of the kitchen.

'And what about Fire Precautions?' asked the Father.

'What about them?' I said to myself. 'I don't expect there are any.' In reply I said, 'Yes, I am worried about them. The present arrangements do not seem very suitable and I am going to get the Fire Brigade up to look at them.'

Needless to say I was delighted when they not only enrolled their daughter, but put the name of the younger one down as well. The word went quickly round the morning tea parties that Craighead was on the upgrade.

So the new girls started coming in, and by the end of the year I had 60 pupils instead of 42, and inquiries began coming in from all over the South Island.

Yet it was no good having more girls if there was nowhere to put them and inadequate room for them to play in. Then suddenly a possible situation appeared. The little house next door which had quite a large garden came up for sale at £1,400. I hastily applied to the Diocese for the money to buy it, pointing out it would be ideal for the younger children who could live there in a home-like atmosphere, and release accommodation for the older girls. One of the Governors and I went up to Christchurch and argued for two hours with the Standing Committee who pointed out all money was needed for Clergy salaries. I came back bitterly disappointed.

Fortunately the member of Governors was Mr Walton and on the way back he saw how upset I was.

'Don't you worry,' he said, 'as a lawyer I know an old lady who was asking me where she could invest some money. I'll try her when we get back.'

He did and she lent the money on mortgage and we were able to buy the house, build two class rooms on it, and move all the small children, twelve in number, over there. An English governess who was looking for a job, took over as Housemistress, and I was much flattered when the Governors called the house after me!

Yet it still grieved me that when I took the parents round, the school was so unattractive with its flaking paint, and worn lino. My First Assistant agreed with me and as there was no money for repairs, we sent the boarders out for a Girl Guide hike, and set to work to paint the bathrooms. It took all day and the Matron was not pleased when the girls came back and several were sick.

'It's all that paint,' she complained, as she returned from her day off. 'How you got the painters to come in on a Saturday beats me.'

'More likely the dampers they cooked on the hike,' I said.

After this the girls went out all day on a Saturday and the 'painters' moved in. In my second term I moved my sitting-room to a larger more attractive room on the north side, and turned the old one into a library. It took several Saturdays to paint it all cream, but it made a more attractive room to greet Parents when they came to look at the school. We also made curtains and new bedspreads in our spare time, and I learnt to mend some of the springs in the old iron bedsteads on which the girls slept.

There still remained the roof, and every time I saw it I thought how it spoiled the look of the school as it was of corrugated iron, and was rusty in places. Finally I could bear it no longer, and during the holidays borrowed a long ladder and sitting astride the roof started to paint it a nice red colour.

It was then that the Bishop arrived and was not pleased. It was the only time I saw him really angry.

'What on earth are you doing up there, Miss Oakeley,' he called. 'Come down at once or you will be killed.'

'I can't stand this rusty old roof any longer,' I replied, and swished a great blob of paint across the eaves.

'Please come down,' he pleaded. 'It is not only undignified for Headmistresses to paint roofs but also extremely dangerous.'

'I can't,' I replied. 'I've begun now and it will look awful if I stop.'

It looked like a deadlock but the Bishop suddenly changed his mind.

'If you will come down with great care, I will get the Governors to arrange for the painters to finish it,' the Bishop called up. So down I came thankful not to have to do all the work. A few weeks later we had a beautiful new red roof which made the school look quite different, and when parents arrived they saw a smart red roof sparkling in the sun.

But I always thought the future of the school was tough, and in those first four years disaster nearly overtook me. I realise in those early days that one false move, one mistake would be attributed to my lack of experience, and could ruin not only the school but my own career.

The catastrophe which nearly wrecked everything took place soon after my arrival. The girls had been out with their Parents, and we were regaled at supper with their adventures, and all they had had to eat. So we were not surprised when Georgie and Janet, who seemed to have excelled themselves, were sick all night. By midday a rather white faced Janet returned to school but Georgie continued to be sick. When I went up to see her she was drawing her legs up and down in a rather ominous way.

'Hadn't we better call the doctor?' I asked the Matron.

'Why, no,' she replied. 'Just a bilious attack. She has no temperature. In fact it's subnormal.'

I felt vaguely worried still, and after going downstairs for a while went to look at Georgie again.

'Are you in pain?' I asked her.

'No, I just feel uncomfortable,' she replied.

I saw the Matron again.

'I think we must have a doctor,' I said.

'It's no use,' she replied. 'Georgie's doctor has gone to the war, and I doubt if you will get another. Look, I know the child is all right and if you are not going to trust my judgment, you had better find another Matron,' was the reply.

I went downstairs again. Then I made up my mind.

'Look,' I said, 'I know you consider there is nothing wrong with Georgie but I just feel we must have a doctor.'

So I rang one of the other doctors who kindly said he would come up straight away. I apologised for calling him, and sure enough he only spent a few minutes in the sick-room.

'I'm sorry,' I ventured, 'but it is a responsibility having other peoples' children in your care.'

The doctor paused a moment.

'Miss Oakeley,' he said, 'that appendix has burst. I am just going to get a rug out of my car, and then I shall take Georgie to the hospital as fast as I can.'

I rang the parents and they came in, and sat up all night waiting for the phone. By morning Georgie was a little better, and after a slow recovery she was able to go home, but it had been a near thing and might have ended my career at Craighead abruptly.

After this I engaged a trained nurse which was just as well as I found New Zealand girls were very prone to appendicitis. This relieved the Matron and myself of all responsibility and was essential as the school became bigger. In later years I met Georgie in Christchurch with her husband and family and reminded her how she had nearly put an abrupt end to my career!

Chapter 11

Holidays

I could see quite early in my time in New Zealand that holidays were going to be a problem. I could not stay at school by myself, and yet I had no house of my own or any relatives in the country. It was true I was always welcome at Bishops' Court, but it was a very busy household and I did not want to impose on the Bishop and his sister too much. The only introduction I had was one from the Victoria League for whom I had often worked in England, taking parties round Oxford. This was to a Lady Ferguson in Denedin, wife of Sir Lindo Ferguson, a famous eye specialist who had me to stay for a week in my first holidays. Curiously enough, Oscar Natzke was singing in Dunedin and we went to hear him. Then I went on to meet Old Girls in Invercargill, recruiting for new girls. On the way I was thrilled with the beautiful Otago and Southland countryside.

Yet I need not have worried about holidays after that. The New Zealanders are the most hospitable and kind people in the world, and I had many invitations. I went to many lovely and interesting places – to Pigeon Bay, where the Hays had settled before the First Four Ships brought the original emigrants; to Blue Cliffs, famous South Canterbury Sheep Station, where one of its great historians entertained me; and down to Glenary, where I learnt to improve my riding and to see New Zealand Station life at its best.

I had always loved mountains, and had enjoyed many Swiss holidays, and now Timaru was on the way to Mount Cook, and the long stretch of the Southern Alps. I promised myself I would try to cross the Southern Alps by all the well-known routes while I was in New Zealand. The beginning, was, of course, the world famous New Zealand Route across the Milford Track. In those days there was no Homer Tunnel so you had to do it both ways, spending two nights on the way.

We started by going through the Routeburn where I was initiated into hiking in New Zealand. I had bought a large pair of mountain boots and duly rubbed them with dubbin, and had filled my haversack with tins of delicious food. After a few miles we met some hungry mountaineers, and I emptied my pack for their benefit!

The Milford Track was beautiful, with lovely mountain flowers all the way. It was only spoilt by the clouds of sand-flies who even descended in hordes when we had a shower at the first huts. The views from the Mackinnon Pass, and at Milford itself were breathtaking, and I was thrilled to have achieved it.

However, I wanted to do something more exciting, and spent the next Christmas holiday at the Hermitage, Mount Cook. One of my Staff was with me, and we decided we wanted to go over the Copeland Pass to the West Coast. On New Year's Eve there was a dance, and I found the man with whom I was dancing was a mountain guide.

'I want to go over the Copeland,' I hazarded, 'would you take us?'

'How much climbing have you done?' he asked,

'Oh, I've often climbed in Switzerland,' I replied, 'but nothing very big.'

'Well, Franz and I are going over to the West Coast tomorrow,' said Mick. 'If you can be at the Hooker Hut by 9am you can come with us.'

Greatly excited we went off early to bed, got up early and packed our haversacks, which an elderly climber made us unpack and checked everything in them, making us take more warm clothes. Then we hurried off and got to the Hooker Hut as arranged by 9am. But no guides turned up.

At last, when we had almost given up hope of them turning up they arrived at 4pm having been sleeping off the party. They were accompanied by a gentleman called the Woman Hater who looked at us with disgust.

Off we set at tremendous pace up a very steep rocky slope until we reached the snow line where we roped up. The Woman Hater and Jean with Franz, and me with Mick. I had never been on a rope before and when I found the going hard gave it a pull, and brought Mick, cursing and swearing down on top of me. The other three had several halts but every time we caught up. Franz said, 'Good we can now go on,' and Mick and I got no rest at all!

Eventually we reached the top of the pass but there was not much view. We slid down the great screes in pouring rain and eventually at 9pm reached the Douglas Hut.

'I have never been so tired, wet and hungry in my life,' I gasped as we fell on our bunks. The guides made us some soup and we fell asleep only to be woken by rats running over us!

Next day we went on at a cracking pace as the guides were due at the

West Coast and wanted to do the trip in two days instead of three. We hurried past hot pools and reached the Fox Hotel in the late afternoon having done forty-two miles in two days. The guides were going back over the Graham Saddle but I had had enough and was glad to spend a few days exploring the West Coast.

Soon to the other passes. Arthur's and the Lewis Passes could be crossed by road, and the Harper Pass was easy going. There we met some deer-stalkers, who let us go out with them provided we ate a deer-stalker's breakfast which proved to be boiled macaroni. When the first deer was shot I could not bear it and we went on.

Another famous pass was Jacks and Jollies, an eighteen-mile trek over the foothills from Hanmer. All these trips could be done without a guide, and we only once struck trouble.

Two of us were exploring the Tasman Glacier, and had for once engaged a guide, but he got annoyed with us because we kept on stopping to admire the view, and jumping on patches of pink snow.

'You go on,' we said, 'and let us enjoy ourselves as we like,' and he did.

When we reached the De la Beche hut, one of the leading members of the Dunedin Mountaineering Club was there.

'You have no business to come up here without a Guide,' he said, 'and I saw you jumping on that pink snow which is above some crevasses.'

We explained about the Guide, and listened from the women's bunk room while the Guide received a dressing down for abandoning us to our own devices.

But perhaps the most exciting of all the Alpine crossings was going over the Haast Pass. In those days there was no road, and when I later visited New Zealand and there was one, I was amazed at what we had done.

We got a lift to the Fox Glacier from where the track started. There we met the most famous of all the New Zealand Guides, Peter Graham, famous for his climbing with Freda du Faur, and one of the conquests of Mount Cook. He took a very dim view of us setting off on our own.

'I think you should take a Guide,' he protested. But we knew there were none at the Fox at that time and anyway we could not afford it. Some people went over on horseback, but that was out too, so we promised to let Peter Graham know when we arrived and started off.

Helen was carrying forty pounds and I was staggering under thirty-two. I was only allowed to rest every twenty minutes, and it seemed like eternity. However we did the first ten miles and reached the first hut which we were rather surprised to find was occupied by a dapper little man who seemed to know we were coming.

'How did you know to expect us?' we asked.

'The bush telegraph told me you were coming, and supper is ready, venison and cabbage and potatoes grown in the garden,' he replied.

We were rather taken aback especially as the hut only contained one room. However we enjoyed our meal and spent a rather fitful night keeping one eye open occasionally to see he was still in his bed! Next morning we had cold venison for breakfast, and discovered our host was a workman employed on the survey of the proposed road, and he kindly carried our packs up to the top of the pass which was a relief.

We reached the next hut in the early afternoon and this time again found it occupied, the occupants being two villainous looking men who did not appeal to us, so we pushed on to the Blue River. Here the hut was occupied by a handsome gentleman called Joe. We discovered he was a deserter from the New Zealand Army and was making a fortune by selling venison and whitebait. We asked him to telephone a local farmer, Mr Cron whose job was to ferry people across the Haast River. We had been unable to use the phone further back, and Joe told us he had removed the batteries for his own use, and duly phoned Mr Cron and arranged for him to pick us up next morning.

When morning came we said goodbye to Joe and set off for the Haast River ten miles away. It was quite difficult to find the path, but we eventually reached the Haast River at 8.30am and sat down to wait for Mr Cron. And wait we did, all day, eaten by sand-flies and no Mr Cron appeared. As it grew dark we got frightened, as we had no tent and the nights could be cold, and Joe had told us there were a lot of deserters about. Only a few weeks before some nurses had died on the Copland.

'I'm sure we shall die if we stay here,' moaned Helen.

'I think we shall have to go back to the last hut,' I agreed.

So we set off in the pitch dark, though Helen had a small torch and we had the sea on our left. It was pouring with rain and we were cold and hungry, and our packs felt heavier than ever. Eventually at 11pm we saw a light in the distance.

'Joe, Joe,' we called, and a figure came out cursing and swearing. We ran to him like a pair of frightened children and poured out our story.

'What you girls need is a strong cup of tea,' he said, and led us into the hut where we saw a Maori telegraphist sitting up in bed.

'Excuse me getting up to greet you ladies,' said the Maori gentleman, 'but I have taken off my trousers.'

Thankfully we gulped down cups of tea while Joe told us he had been to Wellington once to stay in a hotel but the beds were too soft and he had to sleep on the floor.

Next morning we were off again, this time accompanied by Joe riding his horse. Old Cron duly arrived with the boat, and said he had had to go mustering the day before and so could not come. He helped us into the boat and the horse was tied on behind and away we went at top speed down the Haast River. Half-way across the horse tried to get into the boat and we thought we were going to turn over but Joe pushed it back and in spite of all we arrived safely on the other shore, fetching up on a sandback. We said goodbye to Joe, and accepted Mr Cron's offer to go and have a cup of tea with his wife.

'I don't think you girls should be hiking about on your own,' said Mrs Cron. 'There are a lot of bad characters in this district. I hope you did not come across a man called Joe who is a deserter, a regular crook, and God knows what else.'

We did not say we had had two nights in his hut, but thanked her politely and went on our way up the other bank of the Haast. By now it was raining heavily and we had great difficulty getting over the creeks. Fortunately we had a length of rope, and one went across with it round the waist, and the other followed.

Eventually we reached the top hut where we were supposed to cross the Haast again but all the rain had caused it to flood and become impassable. I was getting agitated about school but fortunately an English girl and her Australian guide arrived. He was a very tall man and he was able to get across. We clung round his neck and floated behind and just managed to reach the other bank. By now we were very short of food.

We now had a twenty-five mile hike down to Wanaka which was made worse by Helen putting her knee out and having to put it back at intervals.

Just when we were rather desperate we arrived at Wanaka Station and found someone was just about to drive down to the town of Wanaka. When we got there we went round to a friend's house, but found they were at church so contented ourselves by frying eggs and buttering bread as we were quite famished.

Next day as we went back by bus to Timaru we looked at all the huts and said, 'Did we rally sleep in places like that?'

And when we did get to Timaru we bought two tea-towels and posted them to Joe, so he did not have to dry the plates on his trouser seat any more!

Later on I had a little car called Mickey Mouse and a small tent and was able to spend holidays going all over New Zealand, even to Cape

Reinga, at the very top, and before I left the country there was no part I had not visited.

Chapter 12

Government House

Meanwhile the school was beginning to flourish. It was not, of course without many disappointments and frustrations but little by little the numbers rose, all the dormitories were reopened and we began to find ourselves short of accommodation.

It was then that I got an urgent phone call one morning.

'This is the ADC to the Governor-General speaking. Is that Miss Oakeley? Their Excellencies would like to visit your school this morning on their way from Dunedin. Would it be convenient?'

I hastily said it was, and rushed off to get organised. School was immediately stopped, and all the younger children were sent to weed the front borders; the older ones were told to pick flowers and put them in pots over the holes in the linoleum; and the Staff were asked to see all the rooms were tidy and to make themselves presentable.

The new Governor-General, Sir Cyril Newall, and his American wife had only recently come to New Zealand. He had been Marshal of the Royal Air Force, and we knew they had three children – two girls and a boy.

Precisely at 11.30 the Governor-General's car arrived, and Sir Cyril and Lady Newall stepped out. They told me that while they had been in Dunedin they had met Lady Ferguson and she had suggested they visited the school on their way north.

How glad I was I had my nice new drawing-room and did not have to entertain their Excellencies in that dark back room! After some conversation, Lady Newall asked to see the school and we started to go round. She seemed pleased with everything but I was only too aware how restricted and poorly furnished it was after the English school where her daughters had been.

When we got into one of the dormitories, Lady Newall sat down on one of the beds and I prayed silently it was not one with a hole in the middle. She turned to me and said, 'Miss Oakeley, I have decided to send my younger daughter to your school. The older one will go to the North

81

Island and the younger to the South Island and that should please everyone. They are very close to each other in age and I prefer them to be separated.'

I tried not to say 'Yes' too quickly, and then in five minutes it was all settled and the Governor-General's car disappeared down the drive, leaving me bewildered and astonished. Nevertheless the enrolment of Diana Newall as a pupil was a great help because it proved that Lady Newall was not only trying to please the South Island but she had chosen Craighead from a number of excellent other schools in it. If the school was good enough for the Governor-General's daughter, it was good enough for South Island girls.

The news spread rapidly, and generally caused some amazement. Immediately, we were inundated with requests for places and for the first time I could pick and choose, even turning down some who had gone to other schools and now wished to return!

When Diana arrived we started with a sea of troubles. First she developed a red patch on her cheek and rather to my horror it turned out to be ringworm. However, when I rang Government House, they were quite cheerful and said she must have caught it from the Government House cats! Then she went riding and fell off her horse, getting slightly concussed, but apparently this had happened before and no one worried about it either.

With Diana at the school we saw a lot of the Governor-General and Lady Newall. No one could have been more understanding or co-operative as parents. In 1941 Lady Newall presented the prizes and while Diana was at school they often came to Sports Day. Finally when eventually we did start the Chapel Lady Newall came specially to lay the foundation stone.

It was not easy for Diana to come to a new school in a strange country and to find herself the centre of attention. She was a clever girl, devoted to animals, but very shy and found it embarrassing that everywhere the school went, people wanted her to be pointed out, and if possible to meet her.

I well remember the occasion of the Boys' High School Dance, when Diana did not want to go because she hated being the centre of attention and only agreed when it was pointed out, it was letting her parents down to refuse to go.

The family had a small dachshund called Heinkel who was Diana's special pet and usually came down with Sir Cyril and Lady Newall when they were visiting the school. After one Sports Day a rather distraught ADC came to see me at 9pm to say Heinkel had disappeared and their

Excellencies were very concerned. We searched the school grounds and even went to the park where the sports had been held, but no Heinkel.

Then I had an idea. 'We had better search the dormitories,' I suggested.

Of course, when we got to Reynolds Dormitory where Diana slept there was Heinkel sitting up in her bed, with his little paws over the sheet. He was promptly removed and taken back to the hotel for the night.

Perhaps as a reward for having Diana and looking after her, I was invited to stay at Government House in Wellington for a week. It was almost like going to Buckingham Palace! In the evening we all wore long evening dresses and long white gloves. Unfortunately I had no long gloves but the kind lady-in-waiting lent me hers. We waited in a circle until their Excellencies came in and then all curtsied or bowed, and followed them into the dining-room.

I enjoyed very much having the Government House car and chauffeur complete with Union Jack and the New Zealand Standard, to go shopping or sightseeing. Diana and her sister were excellent hostesses and took me all over Wellington which they were beginning to know well. Like Sydney it had a lovely harbour, and was known as Windy Wellington, where no one could keep an umbrella up.

My last episode with their Excellencies was just before they left. The lady-in-waiting was ill, and Lady Newall asked me if I would go to Palmerston North with her, acting as lady-in-waiting. She wished to go to a nursery to buy some plants.

We set off in the official car with the flag flying.

I had been instructed in the way to behave. 'Take a pair of spare nylons, and some money in your bag in case of need,' and I duly did.

We had not gone very far when Her Excellency saw a beautiful garden on the side of the road, and told the chauffeur to stop.

'What a lovely garden!' she exclaimed. 'Please go and ask the owner if I can see it.'

So in I went and knocked on the door. There was a long pause and then a voice called out, 'Sorry, not at home. I'm busy.'

I knocked again and she shouted, 'Who is it?'

'It's me,' I answered. 'The lady-in-waiting to Lady Newall, the wife of the Governor-General and she has seen your garden from the road, and would like to visit it.'

'You'd better come in,' the voice said, and added, 'I've just washed my hair.'

So in I went and there was an elderly lady with dripping wet hair lying in front of a heater.

She got up and looked at herself in the glass. 'I can't see her like this!' she expostulated.

'Get a hat and shove your hair in it,' I suggested. She soon found one and bundled her hair inside. I went out to fetch Lady Newall who enjoyed seeing the garden and was much amused when I told her the story of the wet hair.

On we went, accompanied by the Government House Pekinese and one of my jobs was to take it for walks at intervals. When carrying it I was instructed not to crush its legs which were beautifully curved. This was not easy as there seemed to be a lot of large fierce dogs about. Terrified there might be a fight, I hastened to pick up the Pekinese every time one appeared and clutched it amid a hiss of canine protest. I was terrified I might return from the little walk either with a mangled body or a Pekinese with bow legs.

Another of my duties was to find cloakroom accommodation at hotels en route. Most of them took the view that they did not care to have people using their facilities without having a meal and were not impressed by the fact that the visitor was the wife of the Governor-General.

However, we reached Palmerston North safely, collected the plants and had a safe journey back, with the Pekinese tired after all its exercise sleeping quietly in the back of the car.

In 1944 the Governor-General and Lady Newall left New Zealand at the end of their tour of office and of course Diana went with them. She had almost finished her school career and had made many New Zealand friends. Certainly her presence at the school, and the confidence of her parents had been a great help to me.

Diana, was not, however, the only English girl we had in school. For many English parents and for those New Zealanders living temporarily in England the war presented a great problem. Should they keep their children with them and perhaps all die together, or should they be sent a long and dangerous journey to friends or relatives in New Zealand?

A considerable number faced the journey and came. Among them was a charming girl called Rosemary who was invited by the Port Line to come to Port Line hosts in New Zealand. Unfortunately the people who had sponsored her were unable to have her and her brother after all, and the two children were stranded. The Managing Director of one of the big shops took the boy, and I was asked to 'adopt' Rosemary for the duration of the war. The Craighead Parents kindly invited her in the holidays and when the war was over she was very reluctant to go home. Later on she wanted to come back again but I suggested she trained for some career first, before taking such a step.

The parents of children who had gone overseas had many problems when they got back. Often the separation had lasted five or six years and the girls were quite out of touch with their parents when they got home. After a free and easy life in New Zealand, riding ponies, camping and swimming, a return to the restricted life in a big English city presented many problems.

Yet they were a great asset to the school because at this time New Zealand was very cut off; news was very censored; and letters infrequent. The English girls were able to talk about a different world, different homes and schools; and a way of life which was unlike that in New Zealand. Before this their knowledge of England was what they had heard from their grandparents, and this was mainly life in Edwardian or even Victorian times. But the evacuees benefited enormously from their stay in New Zealand becoming more self reliant and copying the easy, happy ways of their New Zealand friends. It made a bond between girls on different sides of the world when the war was over.

Chapter 13

Wartime

All this time the war had been continuing. People often told me afterwards I was lucky to be out of the war zone during those years, but most of them knew nothing of the war in the Pacific. New Zealand had sent all her Expeditionary Force overseas, and did not withdraw it from the Middle East when the Japanese came into the war. Rumour said the country had one anti-aircraft gun in Auckland, and the threat of Japanese invasion was very real. It was only the battles of Coral Sea and Midway Island which saved New Zealand.

It was quite early in the war that the horrors of it were brought home to me. One of the parents, who originally came from Great Britain, had tried to join the New Zealand Forces without success as he was too old. So he decided to go home to Britain and join the British Forces.

He came to see me before he left and promised to go to see my Parents in England, but when he got home the British Army would not have him either. So he got a job in a munitions factory and kindly called on my parents on the way south.

Two nights later there was a raid on Plymouth and he was killed. His wife rang up to tell me and as she was out in the country asked me to tell her daughter. I was appalled and had no idea how to do it. She rang twice more to ask if I had done it, and eventually I sent for the girl and told her. As the war went on it became a more frequent occurrence. Nevertheless I always felt inadequate and dreaded having to do it.

As the war went on and the threat of Japanese invasion came ever nearer, it was obvious we would have to decide what to do if the Japanese did land. Elaborate plans were made to evacuate the school by bullock wagon to an inland sheep station where the proud owner had a World War One cannon to defend us. We had several attempts at evacuation, but it never actually took place. It was decided that if there was a Japanese conquest, it would be better to be in a town rather than go out into the country. The Japanese would probably appoint a Governor for each town, while the countryside would be at the mercy of roving bands.

In case of bombing we were asked to get all the girls under the dining-room tables, with a jujube in their mouths to prevent shock. On one occasion a Japanese submarine was rumoured to be in Timaru harbour and we all went into the dining-room as arranged.

'Please may I have another jujube. I've eaten mine,' was the cry all round.

The war brought great shortages of manufactured goods to New Zealand. Before 1939 there was little manufacturing done. For instance the raw wool went home to England and was manufactured there and made into cloth, which was then sent back. Soon we were short of everything, cups, cutlery, clothes. These were some of the many things which had been exchanged for New Zealand butter and cheese. Rationing of a kind was introduced but it was not very stringent. However, by the end of the war New Zealand was starting to manufacture all types of goods, beginning with New Zealand made cups which were incredibly bad. They were handed out at the railway stations and were made of earthenware without handles.

For most English people in New Zealand at this time the lack of communication was the worst problem. There was, of course, no television and the radio was poor. Night after night we heard the Home Counties had been bombed and we wondered exactly where they were. Many letters were lost at sea and months went by without my knowing what was happening to my family.

The only way people in New Zealand felt they could help was by sending parcels overseas, but even this had its problems. They were very expensive and often did not reach their destination, either being sunk or stolen en route. One year a ship came in and the Captain offered to fill his freezing compartments with turkeys for Christmas. There was great excitement and, like everyone else, I bought a huge and very expensive turkey and paid another large sum for the ship to take it to my Parents. We heard afterwards they were all sold when the ship reached Southampton and none of the proposed recipients ever received them.

When Singapore fell, my brother and brother-in-law became prisoners of the Japanese in Changi Camp and it was a long time before we knew they were safe. I think I was probably the first to know where they were, when I received a call from a man in Invercargill.

A voice said, 'Is that Miss Oakeley? I have just been listening to Tokyo Rose, broadcasting from Tokyo, and she said your brother Rowland Oakeley and your brother-in-law, Mervyn Sheppard were safe in Changi Camp in Singapore. We have been asked to give Miss Oakeley in Timaru this news.'

I was astonished to hear this and wondered how the news had come through, and found the caller was a man who had been badly wounded in World War One and was now bedridden. Unable to sleep he listened to all the broadcasts of Tokyo Rose and took down the lists of prisoners as they were read out. I immediately cabled home and they were much relieved to get the news.

Later the same man rang again and said my brother-in-law was appealing for insulin for a diabetic prisoner, but although I contacted the Swiss Red Cross, they were unable to help.

As the war progressed the American offensive in the Pacific began and hordes of Americans came to New Zealand. Many were suffering from malaria, and stayed until they had recovered. New Zealand was a temporary base for the Americans before they moved on to Australia. Up to that time New Zealand had looked to Britain and followed British habits and customs, since it had once been a British Colony. They were astonished at the GIs who thought nothing of making new roads over what seemed impassable places; putting new hospitals up in a matter of weeks; and spending money lavishly wherever they went. Nylons were handed out to all who wanted them, and New Zealanders learnt new words, and new customs. But the Americans hardly seemed to have arrived before they were gone and Japanese prisoners came instead. They were put in a camp at Featherston, in the North Island and people made trips up to see what they looked like!

Meanwhile, the New Zealanders were part of the 8th Army and everyone thrilled to hear about the part they played in the Battle of El Alamein and the great advance across North Africa. Captain Charles Upham was to win the only double VC in the Western desert, and was the only living man to hold it. In spite of everything, the New Zealand casualties were very heavy and with such a small population of just over a million it was particularly hard for it to lose the flower of its young men.

Naturally labour was very short as well. There were to be no long summer holidays for school teachers or their senior pupils. Everyone was to be called up for eight weeks, and given the choice – a pickle factory, because the New Zealand troops loved pickles, a nurse aide in a mental hospital, or work on a farm.

When the Parents came to collect their girls at the end of term, 'I just feel I can't do any of these things,' I moaned. 'I'm always so tired at the end of term, and to work all the holidays would be too much.'

At this one of the Parents came up. 'Actually,' she said, 'I could do with some help on the station. My husband has not recovered from his stroke, and I don't know how we shall manage.'

'I'd love to come,' I said, 'but I've never done any farming. I suppose I could learn?'

The station was Glen Lyon right at the back of the Mackenzie Country. In those days it was very isolated. Stores came in once a year, and to get there they had to go by truck to Lake Ohau; go across by boat; and then be picked up by truck the other side. The homestead itself was at the end of a long valley. My hostess had been a town girl and had adapted herself to life on an isolated station most wonderfully in a situation where she had to send her three children to boarding school. She once was faced with a group of the dead bodies of youths from a climbing accident who were brought into her kitchen.

The first morning we had to be up at six and catch the horses. There were three children – Joan who was at school with me and the two boys who were younger. My experience of riding was that, either the horses were brought round saddled and ready to ride, or you held out some oats and they came meekly. These horses were away on the horizon.

'How do you catch them?' I asked Joan.

'Oh, they'll come,' she said, but I had to bribe one of the small boys to catch mine!

By some miracle I managed to get on, and off we went jumping over tussocks and leaping across small streams. I came off three times on the way out, but no one seemed to care and I had to get on again somehow.

We found the merino sheep at the head of the valley and drove them back slowly to the homestead. The old ewes kept on lying down and had to be picked up and laid across one of the horses. When it was my turn I got the sheep across, but it fell off and I had to start again.

We deposited the sheep at the shearing sheds where professional shearers took over. I was told to act as a sweeper up, and this took all day, until the sheep were shorn and ready to go back to their pasture. First they had to be watered from a watering can so that they would not catch cold. The shearing had been with blades so that the wool was not cut too closely.

When the sheep were ready we took them back to the pasture at a slow pace, and then to my horror Joan said, 'And now we go full gallop for home.'

It was a terrifying chase, and I clung on for dear life only thankful I had not got an English saddle but one with a high pommel which helped me to cling on.

I arrived at the homestead absolutely exhausted, and could only think of falling into bed, but my host was waiting. 'Oh, Miss Oakeley, I am so glad you are back,' he said. 'I thought we could have a nice game of bridge!'

Gradually I got hardened, and was able to enjoy the great thrill of mustering some cattle. They were far up the valley, and we rode up about six miles to fetch them. Joan was on a big horse and was wielding a stock whip. I thought how stupid she was at school, and made no progress with her lessons, and shamefacedly realised it was I who was so stupid on this occasion.

We rounded up the cattle, and had to swim them over a river which was most exciting. Then we drove them down the valley. I was on the outside and every time a cow strayed I had to go after it, and of course when the horse swerved I came off. Eventually we got them down and into a sort of corral, and again came the fast gallop home – but I was getting better.

On another day I was sent with the two small boys to divert the creek. It crossed the road on the far side of the bridge and we were told to divert it under the bridge. We had a lovely day, wading in the water, and eating our sandwiches at the side of the creek. Full of pride at a good job done we came back in the evening, only to find we had diverted it the other side of the bridge, and it was threatening the homestead garden. Needless to say we were not popular.

We worked every day except Sunday, and I soon began to toughen up. At any rate I felt I had done my share of war work and went back to school a deep brown colour, and far from being exhausted, had never felt better.

So the war went on until one night coming back from the pictures with the doctor and his wife, we turned on the radio. The reception was very bad but we could just hear: 'Landed early this morning–weather forecast doubtful–number of casualties–ships crossing the Channel–General Eisenhower in command . . .' and we knew D-Day had begun.

It was the beginning of the end, and I thought how I had done more than the four years of my contract, and perhaps I could soon go home.

Chapter 14

Home Again

By the end of 1944 it was obvious the war in Europe was coming to an end, and I was anxious to go home. I had done five years, and letters from home told me my Mother was not too well and I ought to go back. However, it was still quite dangerous to travel and it was almost impossible to get a travel permit. It was only by the efforts of the local MP that I managed to get a passage. A retired Head took over the school and in January 1945 I left New Zealand. I was sad to say goodbye to the Archbishop (to which title the Bishop had succeeded) and his sister, and I prayed with them in the Bishops' Court chapel before I left.

I sailed from Wellington, escorted to the ship by the Government House ADC and found myself in an eight-berth cabin with seven elderly ladies, most of whom went to bed at six. The porthole was hermetically sealed, and there were constant complaints about my coming in late. As far as Panama we were all right, but after a most interesting passage through the Canal we went up to New York to join a convoy and had a most hair raising trip across the Atlantic.

Each night a few tankers disappeared and the convoy got smaller and smaller. I was too frightened to stay below as we had no hope of survival if we were hit, so I slept on the deck the whole way across.

Soon we reached the coast of Ireland and everyone was wondering at which port we would arrive. Some thought it would be Glasgow, others Belfast. However, I knew when we arrived at a port with lock gates that it was Avonmouth as no other port in the British Isles had such things.

Since it was still wartime no one was able to find out when we would arrive or which port it would be and we were surprised to see a lone figure waiting on the dock.

We had a number of New Zealand wives on board who were going to join their husbands. They immediately rushed to conclusions.

'I'm sure MY husband would have found out.'

'He's so clever, he would have been in touch with the Admiralty.'

'I knew Bill would be here.'

As we drew near it was indeed a Naval officer and his wife was overjoyed, but when he came on board he told her he had been living with another woman all the war and had two children by her. It was a sad return for her after a long and difficult voyage.

Hardly had we arrived than the Air Raid Warning sounded and we were hurried off the ship and into air raid shelters in Bristol. Fortunately I had an elderly aunt who lived in Clifton and after the All Clear I managed to get a taxi, and find my way up to her flat. She was very surprised to see me in the middle of the night when she though I was in New Zealand!

New morning I rang my parents and my Mother was overjoyed. My Father was less enthusiastic. 'You have given us a lot of anxiety,' he said. 'You should have stayed in New Zealand.'

And so to my childhood home of The Gables, and back in my own little room with all my possessions around me. Only the orange volumes of the Left Book Club had disappeared. My Mother confessed that in case the Germans conquered the country and put her in a Concentration Camp for having them, she burnt them.

It all seemed so much the same but in reality there were many changes. My sister was living in the village and there was her little daughter the charming Lavender aged three to get to know; and my sister-in-law was also in the village with her twins, who had spent most of the war in South Africa. But their husbands were still in Changi Camp, and the war in the Far East did not seem like ending.

My friends did not seem to have forgotten me! I spent a weekend with Yvonne whose husband was now Medical Superintendent of the TB Hospital at Colindale, and whose little Nicola was my god-daughter. The men at Colindale had been evacuated to Rhyl but they were so homesick they had to be brought back. Soon after their return a party of ATS were sent to an empty wing for the night and were all killed by a bomb.

I also spent a very terrifying night with my friend Horse who had survived the war all the time in London. The Germans were trying to hit Battersea Power Station with rockets that night, and so we spent it under the table.

However, the war was drawing to a close and the day I was going to visit my cousins in Scotland was VE Day. I stood in Piccadilly Circus where all the flags were lying rolled up on the window-sills till the peace was finally declared, and then we danced round Eros, and sang all the patriotic songs. The celebrations continued in the night train to Scotland especially as we crossed the border.

So I spent the summer visiting relations and enjoying a time of leisure.

In August the Atom Bomb was dropped and the Far East prison camps were opened and we got ready to welcome home my brother and brother-in-law.

But there was a long delay. Lists of those who had been freed were read out in Singapore but my brother's name was not on them, and we feared he had died in the camp. We had practically given up all hope, when we got a cable from a cousin in the WRNS in Colombo. 'Had lunch with Rowland. All well.'

Later we found he was so tired of parades and roll calls he went to dig up his silver, and missed the vital one, and a few weeks later we were welcoming him home. My brother-in-law followed later, and we were told he had been badly tortured.

So we were a complete family again, and I was glad this was the year I had returned from New Zealand. Yet many things were changed. Everyone was tired and peace did not bring the changes everyone had hoped for. Clothes and food rationing went on; trains were overcrowded and shops poorly stocked. As de-mobilisation began, so unemployment increased and, as in 1921, disillusionment and depression set in.

There were, however, many things I had missed while I was in New Zealand. It was marvellous to be with my family again, to say what I liked, and to have those round me who loved me, and were glad to have me with them again. I had missed the English countryside and the trees; I had often longed for a misty day during New Zealand's glorious sunshine; and it was pleasant to be able to enjoy village life again.

But, of course I had to get a job. My old Headmistress Miss Ham suggested I took over St John's which had suffered very much from the war. The evacuation had been too late and the school closed after a bomb narrowly missed it. The buildings were all still there, but the price was enormous, and I had to tell Miss Ham I could not afford it. I had little chance of getting an English Headship at 32, and I did not want to go on the staff of a school again.

Meanwhile Craighead seemed to be going well, though I waited for news about the building of the Chapel. The foundation stone had been laid before I left, and I imagined building would have been begun, and it would soon be finished. However, no letter mentioned it.

Then came a cable from the Archbishop.

'Regret the Diocese has decided to abandon the idea of a Craighead Chapel owing to rising costs.'

How wily he was. He wanted me back and he knew this would bring me and in January 1946 I sailed back to New Zealand.

This was a very different voyage from the first one. I knew where I was going; I had many friends there; and I had a mission to complete.

The ship was the *Akaroa* and it was full of English girls who had married New Zealanders and were off to join them. They were very apprehensive about living in New Zealand and glad to meet an English woman who had lived there.

'I wonder if I shall recognise him again?' asked one.

'All I want is a pavement,' said another. 'I want to be able to wheel the baby in the pram.' As she was going to a spot fifteen miles from Te Awamutu in the North Island I thought it was unlikely!

Moreover, I was not on my own this time as I had an English Primary teacher, who was very experienced with me, and I knew how splendid it would be for the younger children to have her.

Next to our cabin was a war bride from Greenock. She had met her future husband when the New Zealand troops landed there, and was now on her way to join him. She had a single cabin which was just as well as she had a beautiful fur coat; a Crown Derby tea set; and a huge trunk full of valuable clothes. I kept in touch with her when we reached New Zealand and was full of admiration for the way she adapted to a totally different life.

Once again we docked at Auckland, but this time there were welcoming Old Girls; and in Christchurch there was the Archbishop and his sister; and so we came back to Timaru to find the drive lined with girls, all smiling and waving and cheering. This time the school was glowing with paint, the grounds were tidy and as well as my lovely bedroom, I had an attractive sitting-room waiting for me.

But as I went up the drive, I looked towards the shrubbery and could just make out a half-buried foundation stone of the chapel, now covered in weeds. This was why I had come back; this was my first priority.

Chapter 15

The Building of the Chapel

Just before I left New Zealand in 1945 the school had acquired another house. This was the property of the Kerr family which lay beyond Oakeley House. I had become friendly with Mr Kerr, and he promised when he died we could have first refusal of the house. Following his death the Diocese bought it for us, after a tremendous struggle.

On the day it became a part of the school everyone lined up by the Oakeley House fence, and each girl rushed at it, and knocked down a section until it was all down. Then they cleared it all away and went and danced on the new lawn. The house was called Salmond House after the second Headmistress who died so sadly, and it became a great asset to the school.

The spacious lawn was made into a hockey field and no longer did the school have to play in the West End Park where the dogs ran away with the balls. I coached all the hockey and soon the team no longer played only the local townships, but ventured to Christchurch and Dunedin to play and often to beat the other Diocesan Schools.

There was also room for three hard tennis courts, and I moved the intermediate girls, the elevens and twelves over to the house to sleep on the top floor; and the Sanatorium and Sister to a flat on the bottom floor. With this acquisition eventually the numbers went up to the full compliment of 220.

Finally, we were able to buy a small bungalow and turn it into a Staff House. So the grounds became complete. It was named after Archdeacon Averill, then Chairman of the Governors.

But there was still the Chapel. Lady Newall had laid the foundation stone in 1944, but since then every possible trouble had occurred.

When I first had the idea I chose a site in the shrubbery, which was an area of trees on the west side of the school. Everyone liked the idea of a little Chapel among the trees but we soon ran into difficulty. The Borough Council announced they could not give building permission as this was the site for a new road, and two other roads to link up with it were planned across the school land. Kind Mr Walton eventually went up to Wellington in 1947, and talked the whole matter over with the Town Planning Board, and a special Commission was sent down to investigate. In their report they stated they considered the proposed roads unnecessary and supported our petition that the area should not be town planned while it was a school. The Borough Council then gave us permission to build.

But our troubles had only just begun. During the long wait the cost had nearly doubled and we had to raise a lot more money. Originally we had started with eleven shillings and seven pence ha'penny and it took great efforts to raise all the money.

Each term when the girls came back they brought money they had earned in the holidays.

'How did you earn this?' I asked.

'I waited by the rabbit burrows, and when a rabbit looked out I hit it on the head, then I skinned it and sold the skin.'

'I cleaned out the hen-house which had not been done for years and Mum gave me a pound.'

'I worked in a shop for part of the holidays and here are my wages.'

So popular was the work scheme that the girls went out working most weekends in term time, and even the Staff handed in sums they had earned. There were too, of course, concerts and bazaars, raffles and sales of work, and gradually the funds grew.

Then of course there were the donations from Parents, Old Girls and friends. One of the most profitable days was the annual Wool Sale. I always awaited it with some anxiety.

'Sorry to tell you, Miss Oakeley, things are not too good and Mary Jane will be leaving at the end of the year.'

Or, 'Well, it's a good year. Here's £50 for your Chapel.'

Some parents gave us fleeces to sell; others gave us eggs and put what we paid in the Fund. Friends in England sent out donations and as the years went by we got some interest.

We were, of course delighted when we got permission to build but then we found that all the wood the builder had stored away for us had been sold and it was impossible to get any more. Again there was a long hold-up, but eventually strings were pulled and we got some.

So, in 1948 building began, but right up to the last minute there were troubles. In the last week before the Dedication there was a builders' strike and the inside painting had not been finished. In desperation I went down to our builder at night; brought him up in secrecy and got him to finish the painting just before midnight.

Next morning we had a great rush. There were the beautiful oak pews, each with a New Zealand flower or bird carved on the end by Mr Gurney of Christchurch and given by the Old Girls, to get into place. There was the altar which was lit by a concealed light and the Cross and candlesticks were in remembrance of an Old Girl of the school. None of the furnishings had to be bought, all were given.

Friday 10 December was an unforgettable day in the history of Craighead School. It was the day when at last, after seven years of hard work, disappointments, and frustrations the Chapel was finished. It was to be dedicated to St Anthony of Padua partly because the Chapel at Woodford House in the North Island was dedicated to St Francis of Assisi, and also as someone wryly remarked, 'He was the Saint specially responsible for finding lost things.'

At 7.30 we heard the Chapel bell for the first time. It had been given by the Overseas Old Girls and was a ship's bell from SS *Zeelandia* which had taken part in the war. For the first time we went down through the shrubbery for a Communion Service in our own chapel, and our hearts were very full. I myself was close to tears!

It was the most perfect summer day and the Chapel was full when the Archbishop arrived. The second service was at eleven o'clock and there were so many people that they had to stand in the shrubbery. The service began with the Dedication of the Font and was followed by the Dedication of the Chapel itself.

In his sermon, the Archbishop reminded us of all the struggles and trials we had gone through. 'Its creation is a wonderful story of what has been done through the difficult and dangerous and anxious years of war and a troubled peace.'

His Grace went on to remind us how every girl had worked towards the fulfilment of this dream, and we could hardly believe it had come true.

With full hearts we sang the hymn 'Now thank we all our God', and then the school walked round the outside singing, 'We love the place, O God.'

Because they had built it themselves the Chapel has always been very dear to Craighead girls. Soon afterwards there were christenings, followed by weddings, and every week there was a Communion on Wednesday morning.

For me it not only fulfilled a dream but it gave me an opportunity to take services, to teach the girls about the Christian religion, and to help to

Dedication of Craighead Chapel by Archbishop West Watson

bring them up in the Christian faith. Though we still went down to St Mary's occasionally and to St John's for morning service, we always had a chapel service on Sunday evenings.

The Chapel was of course too small and later a sanctuary was added, and a beautiful east window put in.

So there it stands among the trees in a quiet part of the school, and twice after I went back to Craighead and I went to Communion in the Chapel. On the last occasion I was sitting at the back with two of the governors and afterwards one of the wives said to me, 'What a beautiful Chapel this is. Do you by any chance know who built it?'

I looked up at it, and said very quietly, ' I did.'

Chapter 16

Pageants

In my early years at Craighead I never seemed to have any free time at all, but after the war was over we were able to get teaching Staff from overseas. New Zealand teachers often went overseas, or refused to teach in a private school. The English teachers did not mind doing weekend duties, and most were responsible enough to be left in charge of the school. After I had done my last piece of building, which was a block of form rooms with central heating (immediately taken out by my successor), I felt I could engage in other pursuits outside the school.

New Zealand's early history was important for the treaty of Waitangi between white man and Maori in 1840, so the Centennial was celebrated soon after I arrived. Between 1940 and 1955 most of the small towns and early families were celebrating their own centennial. It was suggested to me by my friend Airini Woodhouse that I should write and produce a Pageant about her family, the Rhodes who had settled at a station called the Levels which was quite near Timaru.

'You must arrange to have it acted at the Levels,' said Airini, 'and all the famous people in South Canterbury at that time must be in it.

It was easiest to have the Craighead girls in it because it would be easier to rehearse. Many of them were descended from the early settlers anyway and wanted to act the part of their ancestors.

There were a lot of lovely clothes which people had kept from the early days though few of the women's clothes would fit even the 12-year-olds. people came from all over Canterbury to see the pageant and I did the commentary. Airini's granddaughter acted the part of little Willy Rhodes perfectly and the arrival of the sheep at the Levels was well timed.

Naturally a few untoward events happened. The cow which was representing the bullock owned by Mackenzie the sheep stealer behaved very badly and had to be led off; and the Tripp family were annoyed that their granddaughter, acting the part of one of the most famous of the early settlers, her grandfather Charles Tripp, appeared in a check suit and a bowler hat.

Unlike England one never had fears about the weather in New Zealand, and the pageant took place in broad sunshine.

'We must have another, it's such fun,' said Airini.

'Where shall it be?' I asked.

'Waimate will be having its centenary soon. Let's have one there,' she suggested.

Encouraged by the success of the Levels we did decide to do another pageant at Waimate. This was to be a much bigger affair as it was to take all day and be broadcast throughout the South Island. It was much more difficult to do because it was almost impossible to rehearse. We tried on the Sunday but only a few turned up so we had to do it unrehearsed, and the commentator had to hold it together.

However, on the day everyone turned up, most of the women bursting out of their grandmother's dresses. Marvellous old buggies had been resurrected and real oxen had been found to do the ploughing scene.

All the same, the day was not without mishaps. The cattle simply refused to go into the arena, and though as a good commentator I had a fund of short stories to fill in the gaps, they began to run out as the cattle went round and round the outside of the arena in a Calgary stampede. Finally they tore in and raced round the arena and then out of the exit to the delight of the crowd. During the evening several people rang up to know why I was laughing so much at this point!

Later in the afternoon, we enacted the Waimate Bush Fire which had burned down much of the settlement in the early days. There had been a good deal of controversy with the local police as to whether this was safe or not and in the end it was decided it might take place provided the Waimate Fire Brigade were in charge. A splendid fire was duly lit but at that moment the Waimate Fire Brigade was called out to a fire in the town. The fire burned readily and we got rather alarmed, but the Brigade got back just in time to put it out. After this episode we saw the Studholme family who were the first settlers making their home.

Because I enjoyed writing pageants and had a dislike of formal concerts when one child after another plays a piano solo, I was anxious to put on plays at Craighead. I had always thought acting was great fun for children and I soon collected a team to help me. Our first effort was *A Midsummer Night's Dream* acted in the shrubbery, when I was very ably assisted by the dancing teacher.

However, this was not really what I meant to do, so I decided to write a play in which everyone in the school would take part. All the parts would be written to suit the character of the girl who was playing it. This was all right when there were only forty-two in the school but by the time I left, it was most difficult allowing for two hundred-odd on a small stage with inadequate lighting. I little thought then that one day I would write and produce a school pageant for over 400 in my later career!

Being a historian I loved to teach the girls history through the plays and the first one I wrote was called the 'Ti Tree' which told the story of the early settlers. It began in Victorian England with the family deciding to emigrate; then they were seen on the ship; and finally making their home near a Ti Tree which was a sign of good land. Of course the family had to be attacked by the Maoris and suffer other difficulties before they were really successful but the girls loved acting it, and we did it on three different years while I was there.

We then became more ambitious and started doing pantomimes which included singing and dancing. The artists painted the back-cloths, the needlewomen made the clothes, and those who liked hobbies made the properties. The favourite pantomime was *Aladdin* because we had a book of songs by Alec Rowley which fitted it very well. Like all pantomimes it had its dramas and I well remember Aladdin rubbing his lamp and nothing happening as the genie had gone to get a drink.

Aladdin was followed by a double *Cinderella*, one original version, the other a modern version. The two Ugly Sisters enjoyed themselves so much they wanted to have a repeat.

Each year we had to think of something different. One year we did a seafaring play called 'Ship Ahoy' with music again by Alec Rowley and a spectacular water ballet; another year we did 'Robin Hood' with the hero climbing down a rope from the dormitory above and the Merry Men coming in up a hole in the floor; and once we were very ambitious and did a play about Outer Space when the family left in a rocket and visited the Moon, Venus and a variety of unknown planets before returning to their own bungalow.

I think my favourite of all the plays was *Hans Andersen*. Many of the girls had seen Danny Kaye in the film and loved the songs. As the school got bigger we had to decentralise, and each form acted a Hans Andersen story like *The Princess and the Swineherd; The Tinder Box* and *The Three Fearsome Dogs*; and *Little Thumbelina among the Flowers*. We had a girl with a lovely voice that year, and she sang the part of Hans Andersen between the separate stories. One of my memories of Craighead is of the whole cast singing the final chorus.

In writing every play I had to think of one funny part, duets for the two cousins who sang so well together; and a special part for the best looking girl. If there was someone who played the flute she had to be fitted in, and we usually had a large animal in which the two girls who were too shy to be seen on the stage were enveloped.

Yet not all our plays were humorous. Every now and then the school acted a nativity play. The Chapel was not big enough for it, so we did it in the hall. We had a large blue back-cloth with holes for the cherubs to look through. The play started with the younger children doing the Old Testament scenes and the older ones sang the carols and did the nativity scenes. One of the best things about nativity plays was that the costumes were easy as most of the characters wore bedspreads or towels. The plays were certainly a matron's nightmare as she had to collect all the bedspreads, and towels, cups and saucepans, and get the cocoa off some of the faces.

'You're not having Maoris again,' she would moan. 'Last time they used up all the cocoa and no one told me. This time I hear you are having black men and black boot polish is impossible to get off.'

The Matron was always glad when the play was at the end of term, and the parents had to do the cleaning up in the holidays!

One of the occasions when we did a nativity play was almost a disaster. We were doing it at half term and the girls were going home afterwards. It had rained almost incessantly for nearly a week, which was most unusual and there were fears the South Canterbury rivers were rising, so we decided to do the play in the afternoon so that everyone could get home safely.

The hall was packed and we had watched the tableaux and the Old Testament scenes when an AA man came in. 'I have to warn you the Rangatata is in full flood and if you want to get to Christchurch you must go now or you will be stranded.'

Immediately everyone was on their feet. There was no time to say Goodbye. Everyone rushed off still wearing costumes and make-up, packed into their cars and drove off.

Unfortunately it was too late. The heavy rains and melting snow had turned the Rangatata into a raging flood and in spite of having one of the longest bridges in the country was rushing over it and flooding the road. Parents and girls were obliged to spend the night at the pub at the approach to it.

What the landlord thought when they all rushed in I never knew! It must have been quite a surprise to see angels, Roman soldiers, shepherds, wise men and even the Virgin Mary herself, complete with child in her arms suddenly rushing into the inn.

Besides the formal plays at school the girls loved to take part in the

South Canterbury Drama Festival as everyone in Timaru was keen on drama. One of the most successful societies was the Readers who met in each other's houses every week and read a selection of plays both modern and classical. When you first joined as I did, you were only asked to read the maid's part for the first year. Then came the night when you were allotted your first big part and the telephone rang for days and days while people discussed how you had to read it. When the reading was over a lavish supper was provided and each hostess vied with the others. One in particular could only have it when her black grapes were ripe and everyone could feast on them.

Occasionally the Readers produced plays and I remember acting in *The Long Christmas Dinner* by Thornton Wilder. This was in the old Timaru Theatre where it was always rather hard to hear. Someone in the gallery was heard to discuss the matter with her neighbour.

'You can hear Miss Oakeley all right,' she volunteered.

'I should think you could,' her neighbour replied. 'You should just hear her on the hockey field in the West End Park. It's enough to waken the dead.'

But all education is not sitting in the classroom learning and the plays and the drama were an important part of our life at Craighead, and in later years when I revisited New Zealand and went to a gathering of Old Girls it was always the plays which remained in their memories and they certainly stayed in mine as some of the happiest and memorable occasions in my time as a Headmistress.

Chapter 17

Visitors

In my early years we had very few overseas visitors, but as soon as planes began coming, we had many. First there were the flying boats; then the big transport planes; and finally the jets.

At first our contacts were mainly with Australia. Our PE staff came from the Swords Club in Sydney and were exceptionally good, and after the war we got music staff from the Sydney Conservatorium.

As we were always short of domestic Staff we welcomed wandering Australians. One day a large fat cook turned up saying he was an experienced chef, and had we a job for him. As the Matron was nearly at the end of her tether with only a trainee girl of sixteen in the kitchen, we welcomed him with open arms. We were getting a little tired of cold meat, salad and tinned fruit every day, so 'Aussie' was a gift from God.

Aussie soon became a prime favourite. He walked into the kitchen hung up his coat, put on a large white apron and got to work. That night we had a meal we should never forget and next morning he was up early baking hard and filling the school with delicious smells.

For two weeks we lived on the fat of the land. Never had the school had such interesting, well cooked and nourishing food. We had wonderful roasts with fluffy potatoes; exciting soufflés; home-made ice cream, the lightest and flimsiest of pastries; home-made bread which disappeared in a few seconds; and splendid cooked breakfasts which brought everyone downstairs and into the dining-room in record time.

Instead of the girls going along to meals looking gloomy, late for meals, and expecting the usual plain food, they rushed into the dining-room anxious to see what was the latest delicacy Aussie had prepared.

Visitors kept ringing up to know if they could come to a meal and I had a rush of dinner parties when people could hardly believe such delicious food could be produced in the old-fashioned school kitchens.

Throughout it all Aussie remained smiling. He never seemed to want any time off, and he became the hero of the girls, teaching and domestic staff. Nor did he complain about the kitchen or demand new equipment.

However, all good things come to an end, and this one did abruptly after four never to be forgotten weeks.

It was Saturday afternoon, and I was writing a letter home when two scared domestics rushed in. 'Aussie's dead drunk, Miss, and running after us with a carving knife,' they screamed.

I looked out of the back door rather timidly and saw Aussie chasing the cat with a carving knife, so I hastily shut the door. Certainly this definitely needed a strong man. But who? We had no gardener or caretaker or a male member of staff. My only hope was the Board of Governors so I went to the phone and rang the Archdeacon who was their Chairman. There was a pause and then he said, 'I'm afraid I can't come – a meeting, I'm afraid. Try one of the other governors,' he suggested.

However, when they heard what was wanted all the other Governors were too busy and suggested someone at school or the police should deal with the drunken Aussie. Finally I asked the local orthodontist who was also a parent if he would come.

'Why, of course I will,' he said at once. 'Horrid situation for you and you obviously need a strong man. I will come as soon as I have changed from my tennis clothes.'

I waited half an hour. All seemed quiet outside but two frightened maids were still cowering in my sitting-room. The girls were fortunately out and the Matron unfortunately away for the day. At last I heard a car and rushed out.

The gallant dentist immediately took control and advanced on the domestic quarters, with myself a reasonable distance behind, and the two maids behind us. On hearing a new noise, Aussie emerged from his quarters, still brandishing a knife, and swaying from side to side.

'Now my good man, we can't have this behaviour here,' said the intrepid governor in a quiet tone. 'Put down your knife, pack your things and go on your way.'

Aussie stopped in his tracks and glared. 'Who the hell are you?' he demanded.

'I'm a dentist and a member of the Board of Governors, and I am ordering you to leave this school here and now,' was the reply.

Aussie paused, slid his finger along the knife, and fired his parting shot. 'Then why the hell don't you get yourself some decent teeth,' he shouted.

I was always sorry I did not hear the reply, but whatever it was Aussie turned, seeming to know he was beaten and went quietly to his bedroom. We heard a lot of banging and shouting and things being thrown about and then he came out with his swag on his back and the handle of the carving knife sticking out of it. He seemed to roll from side to side as if he was on a ship.

'So long all,' he shouted. 'You'll never have such a dinkum cook as Aussie.'

The dentist and I retired to my room for a restorative drink. I could not have imagined what I would have done without him, and remember the episode of Aussie with great thankfulness.

It was a very subdued school who came back from their outing. They rushed in shouting, 'What's for tea tonight.' When the answer came that Aussie had gone and was on his way, there was a wail of dismay. They sat down to their meal of cold lamb and potatoes with a happy memory of better days and gourmet meals.

But Aussie was not the last Australian to work on our Staff. On another occasion two girls arrived looking for work. So desperate was our situation again that the Matron engaged them at once, the one as a cook and the other as a housemaid.

'Would you like to see them?' she asked.

'I'm terribly busy,' I replied. 'Bring them along tomorrow and I'll see them then.' It was one of the most fortunate replies I ever made.

Next morning Matron was up early.

'There's been terrible trouble,' she said. 'I did not like to wake you but perhaps I should have done.'

'Why, what's happened?' I asked, sitting up in bed and thinking one of the girls had been stricken with appendicitis in the night.

'Those two girls,' she answered. 'After they had finished work here they went into town and picked up two men. They went off in a car with them, crashed into a bridge, and were both killed. I was woken by the police at 3am and had to go and identify the bodies.'

How glad I was that I had not seen them, but the aftermath was pretty grim. It turned out they were both orphans who had been brought up in a Roman Catholic orphanage in Australia. There were no relatives of any kind, so they had to be buried in Timaru, and we had to ask the local Roman Catholic church to arrange it.

The priest rang me and told me they would have the Requiem Mass at the Children's Mass on Wednesday morning and asked me to be chief mourner. I immediately rang one of the music mistresses who was a Roman Catholic and asked her to go with me and show me what to do.

It certainly was an unnerving experience. Dressed in deepest black and with veils on our heads, we arrived at the church and walked up the aisle among rows of children ranging in age from 5 to 11. The two coffins were carried behind us and we were duly presented with a missal and led to the front row. There I stood with my head bowed while the Music Mistress whispered instructions from behind. As I looked at my missal I was interested to see a prayer for the conversion of Protestants and Jews which was duly said.

When the service was over, the priest sprinkled the coffins and we were ushered out of the pew, and followed the coffins to the cemetery for interment. It was an experience I shall never forget.

But of course, the arrival of some of our other visitors was often marked by great happiness.

One of the most famous was Field Marshall Sir Bernard Montgomery who came to thank the New Zealanders for their part in the war. It was snowing hard, and he rode in a tank down the main street. The whole population was there to greet him, and he was presented with a pair of deep-pink long johns made in the local factory. He was immensely pleased with this present and kept lifting the turn up of his trousers to show them off. Later he spoke in the theatre, and it was altogether a great occasion.

New Zealand, of course, had its own great soldier of whom everyone was very proud. This was General Freyberg, who later became Governor-General. I remember listening to a splendid broadcast of his describing the long trek of the 8th Army from Cairo to Italy.

It was not always easy to get famous people to stop in Timaru. When Lawrence Olivier and Vivienne Leigh came to act in *The School for Scandal* we were disappointed they were not stopping in Timaru on their way to Dunedin, so I took the whole school to Christchurch to watch it, one hundred miles each way but it was worth it, as we seldom got a play of any sort in Timaru.

Some years after the war we founded a branch of the Royal Overseas League in Timaru and so we were able to meet many famous people who were visiting New Zealand. There was Admiral Hickie who was responsible for the Mulberry Harbour; Sir Alec Douglas Home who was then in the Commonwealth Office; and Eric Linklater who talked about his books. I was so pleased to be the first President of the League and get an opportunity to meet all these famous people.

The only famous visitor to visit the school was the pianist Lili Kraus. We had a terrible search to find a grand piano for her as the school did not possess one, but eventually located a baby Bechstein which had to be unearthed from a pile of photos!'

Finally there was the visit of the Queen and Prince Philip. New

Visit of Sir Alec Douglas Home, Prime Minister of Great Britain, to the Royal Overseas, Timaru

Zealanders were thrilled about the visit, triumphal arches were erected; the public lavatory was hidden in ferns; and a grand reception was held outside. The Queen was presented with a large cross-stitch picture of Mount Cook, and we all retired to he Grosvenor Hotel where one of my pupils played the National Anthem.

No people were so loyal as the New Zealanders and it was a great thrill to have the Royal Family among them.

Chapter 18

Guiding

In England one of my leisure time activities had been running a Brownie Pack. I was, therefore, very interested to meet Miss Ruth Herrick the Chief Commissioner for Guiding in New Zealand. There was a Guide Company in the school and one of the English staff who had joined us took it over.

Miss Herrick was the life and soul of New Zealand Guiding, and she now made me a most astonishing proposition.

'Will you become Provincial Commissioner for Canterbury?' she asked me in 1946.

I was quite astounded. The Provincial Commissioner was next to the Chief Commissioner herself, and Canterbury was a huge Province, 400 miles from north to south and containing nearly a hundred companies and packs. However it was pointed out to me that the higher rank you had the less you had to do, which I could not really believe. So persuasive, however, was the Chief Guide that I accepted.

It was really quite a job doing it all in my spare time. I had first four, then five Divisional Commissioners under me and so it was possible to decentralise. I did manage to visit every company and pack in my nine years of office, though usually it was easier to meet them at the big rallies.

Of these the most famous ones were on the occasion of the visit of the Chief Guide, Lady Baden-Powell in 1947. While she was in Canterbury I was responsible for her and what a task it was! I despaired of getting her in time. Every old man had either been in the Boer War or in the Scout Movement and wanted to shake her hand. Every elderly woman had been a Guide once and wanted to talk about it. Meals were late in hotels, taxis did not turn up, and there was always a panic.

The worst of all was in Timaru itself. For once we left the hotel for the rally in good time. This particular hotel was in a cul-de-sac and at that moment a laundry van arrived and blocked the exit. The driver disappeared into the hotel, and the Chief Guide's car could not get out. Eventually the driver reappeared and we were able to get into the car and head for the parade, only to be stopped by the police.

'You can't come through here,' said the constable, 'there's a Guide parade on.' And indeed the procession had already started and was under way for the saluting base.

Dead on time Rangers, Guides and Brownies passed the saluting base, boldly saluting an empty stand. When we arrived I apologised to the Divisional Commissioner with a hissed. 'It was a laundry van,' and asked for the parade to be repeated, which it was.

This was followed by the worst fright of all. Mid Canterbury was having a big parade in Ashburton, half-way to Christchurch the next day, and the Chief Guide had gone to stay with friends nearby while I went back to school. Before she left Timaru, I was entrusted with her Personal Standard to keep overnight, and I slept with it propped up at the bottom of my bed.

Next morning I was bright and early only to find I had mislaid my car keys and could not start my car. In spite of the fact that people say you can always start a car with a penknife, the combined efforts of all the prefects could not make it start. I visualised the parade not only without the Provincial Commissioner, but more important without the Chief Guide's Personal Standard.

The only thing to do was to think back, and I sat on the steps and tried to think what I had done on returning the night before. Suddenly I remembered I had taken my dirty hankie out of my uniform and put it in my laundry bag. I rushed upstairs and there was the key. The car was quickly started and I rushed to Ashburton, arriving two minutes before the rally was due to start.

'How nice to see you again,' the Chief Guide said, 'always so punctual, and my Personal Standard unfurled just at the right moment.'

She little knew!

The final rally was in Christchurch and over 500 Scouts, Guides, Brownies and Cubs were brought from all over the Province to Lancaster Park. We had a Commissioner's lunch first and it was obvious Lady Baden-Powell was beginning to get exhausted. It was a quarter to two and we got in the car to go to Lancaster Park when she suddenly turned to me and said.

'My dear, I can do no more. I just can't face a rally this afternoon. I must go back to the hotel and rest.'

My heart sank. I thought of all the months of preparation, and yet I sympathised wholly with her. My mind went back to the time I was teaching at St George's and a girl did not want to do her exam.

'Let's just go and sit in the rose garden then and have a quite time,' I said, and we got out of the car and sat on the seat in silence. After a few minutes she smiled and said, 'My dear, I feel better. Of course I will go. It was just I felt so tired, and thought I could not face another big rally.'

After that awful moment the Rally was a great success, and my admiration for a very great lady has remained ever since.

When she had gone I went back to the hotel to thank the Staff, and a strange man asked me to come and have a drink with him. Since I had always thought the Guide uniform was highly unflattering I was much amused!

I was of course very conscious that I knew less about Guiding than most people in the Province. I, therefore, decided to take my Camper's Licence. This meant going to be tested by Miss Mona Burgin, one of the great figures of New Zealand Guiding, and a very tough examiner.

I certainly enjoyed that camp on the Taeri, enormously, even the day when I had to demonstrate my cooking ability which was nil. I had carefully chosen cold meat for the day, but as luck would have it, it rained and Miss Burgin with a twinkle in her eye ordered not only soup, but doughnuts! I simply had no idea how to make them but with cookery book in one hand and a billy full of boiling fat in the other, I did my best. The doughnuts came out in the most extraordinary shapes, but when Miss Burgin commented on this, I said it was more individual to have them like that and it was the usual English way. I don't think she believed me!

Miss Burgin's *tour de force* was a night alarm. When everyone was peacefully sleeping, a whistle blew and woe betide anyone who could not find their clothes or appeared with a piece of uniform missing. It was school holidays and I was unwilling to lose any sleep, so each night when Miss Burgin looked in to say goodnight she was greeted by an array of clothes and shoes laid out ready. As this happened every night she was unable to have her alarm – the first time in any camp.

Rather to my surprise I did get my Camper's Licence, and now felt I could be on equal terms with my Guiders.

Soon after this I helped at a Provincial camp at Cheviot. The Guider in charge had only one leg and was afraid she might be slow buckling on her artificial one in an emergency.

She must have had a premonition because at 4am we were woken by the trees swaying in a most terrifying way. At first I thought it was wild pigs who had careered through the camp earlier on but the Guides were already out of their tents. 'It's a real dinkum earthquake,' they shouted.

I was quite terrified. I remembered the story in the Bible about the earth opening and swallowing up the three men, and I was afraid the whole camp might disappear. The Guides on the other hand looked on the whole thing as great fun and soon made earthquake badges in which they put a nick every time they survived one.

However, everyone sobered down as the shocks got worse and at eight o'clock the police arrived to see if we were all right. A lot of damage had been done in the small town of Cheviot though no one was hurt. If it had been a densely populated area the casualties would have been heavy.

The young Guider and Pack Leader were very frightened so we sent them into the town to see if they could contact the Guides' parents. Just as they got to the Post Office the whole roof collapsed and they came back even more frightened.

As evening came on the shocks grew worse and the inhabitants of Cheviot decided the Camp, which was just outside the town, was the safest place. I slept that night with an old grannie and a mother and baby in my tent. Next day, however, the police came in again and evacuated the whole area.

This adventure did not put me off Guide Camping but I was rather taken aback when Miss Herrick asked me to be one of the Group Commandants in the Pacific Ranger Camp in the North Island. It was on a splendid site and Rangers came from all over the Pacific, the United States, Fiji, India and Ceylon. Everything was most marvellously organised including providing gumboots for the barefooted Indians.

My friend Helen who was Camp Adviser for Canterbury and I were put in charge of the all-day hike. We decided to take all the camp over the track on Mount Tongariro, where they would see hot pools and geysers, and have a marvellous view of the surrounding countryside. We had been over it the holidays before and found it took about six hours of rough walking.

However, when it came to taking the Rangers over it, it was a different matter. Some of the older Commissioners gave up at the first slope; others handed their packs to us before they had gone a mile; and the barefooted Indians and Fijians were covered in blisters soon after the start. By lunchtime we had only covered a quarter of the way and as the afternoon wore on we thought we should never get back! Shouldering packs, strapping blisters, singing encouraging songs hauling the weary along, we somehow managed to get back to the camp by 9pm. As we arrived the large Maori Guider rushed out shouting, 'Oh, my darlings, are you safe?' and gathered her Maori Rangers to her bosom.

Chief Guide Lady Baden-Powell with Provincial Commissioner Miss Mary Oakeley

Neither of us were very popular for bringing them back so late but we felt rather proud we had brought them back at all!

The highlight of the Camp was the Open Day when the Leader of the Opposition, Mr Nash, and the Governor-General's wife, Lady Norrie visited the camp. Each nationality had to give a display and I found myself, of all things giving a cooking display. I sat up most of the night before learning how to make a Maori oven, and to hollow a loaf out, fill it with mince and put it in the ground. This intrigued Lady Norrie and there was a picture of us looking at the loaf, in all the papers. This amused my friends who were a lot dubious about my cooking.

At the display the Australians were supposed to represent Captain Cook, but New South Wales refused if they had to wear white blouses like the other Australians. They had worn blue blouses ever since Guiding started in Australia, so like Achilles they stayed in their tents.

Altogether Guiding was great fun and I met a lot of interesting people, other than my school friends.

Chapter 19

Home Again

I was fortunate enough to go back home on leave in 1949, and again in 1953. In 1949 I decided to go via South Africa, though everyone told me it was the coldest and most unpleasant way to go. It certainly was the most unpleasant and memorable journey I have ever made.

The difficulties began almost as soon as we left New Zealand. We had on board two New Zealand MPs who were going home to a conference in England. They kept very much to themselves on the voyage to Australia and when they arrived in Melbourne it was discovered the two MPs were still in New Zealand and these two were stowaways. The ship was searched very thoroughly in Melbourne and no one was allowed to go ashore but they had slipped overboard at night and were not seen again.

The chief passengers were the All Blacks, captained by Fred Allen, going to play in England. I was put on the Sports Committee and told to get up a concert before we reached Cape Town. I decided to do Cinderella with Fred Allen as the Prince Charming and the largest of the All Blacks as the Fairy Chorus. It took most of my time rehearsing as it was bitterly cold, and it was impossible to go on deck. The ship went by the Great Circle Route and we crouched over our electric heaters most of the way.

On the night of the performance, it was pouring with rain and all the usual hold-ups happened. Prince Charming was supposed to be wearing a pair of white flannels lent by an old gentleman, but just before the play began Allen arrived shouting he had no trousers.

'I'll get them,' I cried and dashed across the wet deck. My leg shot under me, and I felt the most terrible pain. I thought I had broken my leg but the doctor diagnosed a torn ligament and said I would have to lie up for a week.

It was a bitter disappointment, as I especially wanted to see Cape Town, and I could have wept when I saw everyone go ashore without me. Then I had an idea. What about all I had done for the Girl Guides? Perhaps they could help?

There was a phone on board, and I rang the Guide Headquarters, explaining I was stuck on the ship with a torn ligament.

'Of course,' said a kind voice. 'We'd be delighted to help. One of our hospitality committee will be down with a car right away.'

I got the stewardess to help me down the gangway and armed with a large stick I hopped ashore where a Guide car was waiting. Fortunately it had a large, wide back seat on which I lay, and my kind Guider drove me all round Capt Town. We saw all the African ladies with their flowers round the Post Office; went out to Groote Schur to see Cecil Rhodes' House; and drove round the vineyards further inland.

The Guider did not drive herself but had a coloured chauffeur, and I was rather surprised that when we stopped for lunch he stayed in the car.

'What about the driver?' I asked.

'No, he can't come in. This hotel is for whites only,' said my friend, adding, 'I expect he has brought his own lunch.'

But he had not and went all day with nothing to eat. This was the first time I had met apartheid which was to be such a burning question in South Africa later on.

Next day I had an introduction to some friends of a New Zealand doctor I knew and they kindly fetched me from the ship and I was able to lie on their sofa for the day. It was interesting to hear their views on South Africa. They all had coloured servants who lived in little huts at the bottom of the garden. No Englishmen would have looked twice at them!

The daughter was thinking of going to university in England, 'I think I'd really like an English one better,' she said. 'Because I've seen pictures of English girls at the universities and they can go anywhere they like, even after dark.'

She told me that no white woman could go about alone after dark. Girl Guides had to be fetched by the Fathers from their meetings and the Guiders had to be escorted too.

My hostess drove me back to the ship.

'I don't know how you are going to get back to it,' she said.

We had stopped about a hundred yards from the gangway.

'Oh, I can walk that far,' I protested, 'I'm getting quite good with my stick.'

'Indeed you can't,' said my hostess. 'No white woman can walk that far alone at night. I can't come with you because I cannot then walk back to the car alone.'

We sat wondering what to do, but fortunately a white policeman came up and escorted me to the ship.

The ship sailed late in the evening, but when we got outside the harbour it suddenly stopped. It appeared that a group of South Africans, who had been saying Goodbye to their friends had failed to get off! As the ship had to employ tugs to get in and out of the harbour it was a very expensive business to go back. After some time the Captain decided he could not take them to England so we had to go back into Cape Town Harbour at great cost, and then get tugs to take us out again.

Everyone was beginning to say there was a jinx on the voyage, or perhaps there was a Jonah on board. The passengers were beginning to wonder what was going to happen next.

Between Cape Town and Las Palmas a most extraordinary episode occurred. I woke in the middle of the night, and thought we had run into a storm. The ship was bucketing about all over the place, in fact it seemed to be going round in circles.

There was a man on board who was a deserter from the Royal Navy. He had somehow got out to New Zealand where he had been employed for a time at Government House. Then he was discovered but in order not to create a scandal he was shipped back to England by ordinary passenger ship.

By now he was determined not to go back to a Court Martial in England. He knew from his war experience that all ships had an auxiliary steering in a different part of the ship from the bridge.

So, stark naked, he got into the place, switched the steering over from the bridge and yelled, 'I'm bloody well not going back to a Court Martial in England,' and then turned the ship round and headed it back towards New Zealand.

It was some time before the officers on the bridge realised what had happened, and then as the man seemed completely mad they were afraid to tackle him, in case the ship got completely out of control. Eventually they rushed him and he was taken off and put in the ship's hospital, where he later pulled his whole bed to pieces and unscrewed everything he could find in the cabin.

There was, we heard a difference of opinion between the Captain and the Surgeon over his condition. The Captain thought he was feigning madness to get out of the court martial; the surgeon thought it was genuine. Anyway, he gave the crew a lot of trouble and the last we saw of him was being carried ashore on a stretcher when we reached Southampton. He was heavily drugged if rumour could be believed.

We then went on to Las Palmas where we saw all the Talking Dolls on the quayside, looking just like children. It was pleasant to be on land again and most of us bought beautiful embroidery done by the nuns for which Las Palmas is famous.

Soon after we left we found the ship was very short of linen. No more clean sheets, no table napkins, not even a clean towel. We discovered there was a great shortage of linen needed for their embroidery in Las Palmas, and the crew had made a fortune selling all the ship's linen to the convent!

We wondered what else would happen before we arrived in England but apart from a final gale we arrived without further trouble.

Rationing was still on in England and a New Zealand friend had asked me to take a ham home to her daughter, who was living in England. Then she added, 'as you've been so kind, here is one for you to take to your Parents as well.'

So I had two huge hams, two side of bacon, and twelve pounds of butter. Already there had been trouble about it all going in the ship's refrigerator, and some costly tipping had had to take place. Now I landed it all at Southampton not knowing it was illegal to bring food into England.

When the Customs saw the first ham they immediately told me it was forbidden to bring it in and they would confiscate it.

'I'm afraid I've got some more,' I said, and displayed the rest. As they looked at my luggage they saw a large wooden box, labelled 'Best New Zealand Butter 12 lb,' and immediately there was chaos. Everyone was talking at once and saying how disgraceful it all was, and I should have known the regulations.

'All right,' I said at last, 'give it to a hospital or an old people's home or an orphanage. I don't really care.'

'Oh, no Miss, we're not allowed to do that. The whole lot will have to be dumped in Southampton water.'

I was quite furious. Here was a country with a miserable meat ration and a quite inadequate supply of butter, and here was all this beautiful food going to feed the fishes.

I made one last effort.

'Couldn't I see the Head of Customs?' I asked.

This was allowed so I and the New Zealand girl's husband got into the local taxi which my Mother had sent for me, and with the ham and the butter we drove into Southampton while the rest of my luggage remained behind as a hostage.

When we got there I stated my case.

1. I had no idea these regulations existed or, of course, I would not have brought the food.

2. Neither I or the gentleman with me was going to sell it. I was giving

it to my Parents and he would share it with his wife.

My pleas were effective and after a stern warning never to do it again we were allowed to depart.

The end of the story was rather sad. My elderly Parents gave one look at the ham and said it was much too rich after their wartime diet, and anyway they had no fridge. So it was given to the local butcher who had to be given a piece for himself and the rest was divided between various friends.

Chapter 20

School Affairs

Both the two later leaves were short and filled with interesting events. The Headmistresses Conference; a weekend at the Guide Training Centre at Foxlease; and a wonderful evening at a Commonwealth Ball at Hurlingham when I met the Queen and Prince Philip in 1949; and in 1953 a seat on the New Zealand Stand at the Coronation.

All this time I had been working out a method of running a school. Having had so little experience I had to work out my ideas as I went along. What did one do about punishments for instance? There had been some bizarre methods in English schools and the tawse was still used in Scotland. My idea was to fit the punishment to the crime.

So when I came back late one night and found no one had gone to bed because the clock did not say bedtime, I simply put it on the next night, and everyone, on complaining it was an hour early, received their punishment.

Or there was the time when all the lights were turned off at the main, and bedtime was delayed again. This time my hot water supply in my new little bathroom had gone cold, and the culprits had to boil water downstairs not once but twice and haul it up in pails till my bath was full.

Yet many New Zealand Parents objected to their children being punished at all, and once when I stopped a group going to a film, because they had climbed up on ladders to watch an official lunch in the local hall, there was a fierce outcry.

But the worst disciplinary problem was an occasion when two girls went out to the pictures at night and climbed in up the fire escape. They had gone with one of the day girls and her Parents, and when I saw one of them looking guilty the next day, I boldly asked her what she had done the night before and she confessed.

I had always felt I could not be supervising both night and day and had told the girls that if they went out at night they would be expelled. These were the only two ever to meet this fate, and as they came from two of the most important families in the South Island there was a terrible row. It

122

got so bad I went down to confer with an old and wise Headmistress who lived in Timaru.

'It all depends on one thing,' she said. 'Are they good girls or bad girls? If they are bad girls and have been in trouble before they must go: if they are good girls you must give them the worst punishment you can think of and let them stay.'

'They are good girls,' I replied, and went back to wrack my brains.

Later I sent for them and offered the alternative to expulsion.

'You can both stay here for half term when we go away; you must pay someone to look after you and the school buildings while we are away; and you must meet us with cheerful faces when we get back.'

They agreed immediately and an ex-member of Staff with her baby came to look after them for the week. On our return they greeted us with the remark. 'We have so enjoyed ourselves and had a lovely time.'

One of the girls reminded me when I was last in New Zealand how she had a passion for cutting off people's hair and I made her wear her hat night and day for nearly a term when she cut her own off. I can still remember her sitting up in her bath with her panama hat on!

Sometimes it was difficult to get disciplinary ideas over to the older girls and when a Prefect failed to lock up the school one night, I demoted her although she had given the keys to a younger girl to do it, because she had left something there. This was not popular with the Prefects, but I stuck to it.

Another problem was running away from school. I was woken early by a bus driver saying he had seen two of the younger ones walking along the road to Dunedin in dressing gowns and slippers. When I went to pick them up they were already tired.

'What do you think you two are doing?' I asked.

'We're fed up and going home,' they answered.

'But it's nearly one hundred miles,' I said. 'Why not come back and have some breakfast first and I will put you on the train.'

Gratefully they hopped in the car, and were taken back to the junior house, where they settled down again happily.

A second running away was more serious. One of the new girls disappeared and no one could find her. She had not arrived home; there was no sign of her on the road; and she had not been on the train. We found she was upset at the birth of a baby brother of which she had not apparently been forewarned and had gone off in a fit of jealousy. Eventually we found her living with an old Salvation Army lady who had a bungalow on the Timaru/Dunedin road and had taken her in when she stopped for a drink and had kept her ever since.

But it was not only girls who ran away. Once coming back with the Matron from a late meeting in Christchurch we stopped for a sandwich in a lay-by at a place called Orari. We were chattering away when a little boy, about eight came walking by. I let down the window and asked him if he would like a sandwich.

He hesitated and then came over.

'Climb in the back and have a rest,' I suggested.

Gratefully he got in and we gave him some coffee and sandwiches. I knew there was a boys' prep school nearby so I turned to him and said, 'Are you running away from school?'

There was a long silence and then a muffled 'Yes', and it all came out, how it was his first term, how horrid the boys were, how he missed his dog and his pony, and everything was just awful.

We listened in silence, and then I asked, 'What does your Father do?'

He paused.

'He's away at the war,' he said at last, and then added, 'if he was here he'd stop them teasing me.'

'I don't think he would,' I replied. 'He'd expect you to fight your own battles. A soldier's son is not a coward.'

There was a further silence and then I added, 'How did you get out?' It appeared he had come down the fire escape.

I waited a few moments, and then said, 'How about going back the same way?' To my surprise he agreed. So we drove up to the school, I left the car at the gate, and saw him safely in.

Next morning I rang the Headmaster whom I knew well. 'Miss anyone,' I inquired.

He was completely puzzled and I had to tell him swearing him to secrecy and asking him to sort out the troubles which he gladly did. Years later I was to meet the same boy, now an Old Boy, with his Parents at the School Sports, but there was no sign of recognition.

On the whole, New Zealand girls were very different from English ones. In most homes there was no domestic help and the girls were excellent cooks as well as horsemen. Several times we were without domestic Staff, and a group would go into the kitchen and cook a splendid meal.

I remember once a Parent coming to see me with a complaint. 'How could you tell the girls to write home and thank for their half term weekend?' she asked. 'My daughter came home to find me ill in bed. She cooked all the meals, looked after the baby, and fed the chickens, and then wrote and thanked me for a nice weekend.'

On the whole the girls were less interested in academic work than their English counterparts, and many had only one ambition which was to marry the boy on the farm next door. Not many were interested in higher education, but when they did go on to the universities they did well.

I always thought the most difficult thing with which a Headmistress had to deal was the parent who said, 'But I was at the university; my wife was there too, so there must be something wrong with the school for us to receive a report like this.'

In vain I would point out there was musical ability, or she was outstanding at sport or fastest in the swimming pool, but it had no effect, and this problem came up in every school with which I was connected.

One of the most enjoyable parts of school life at Craighead was the school functions. The most popular was the Sports Day, which was first held in the West End Park, and later on our own playing field at Salmond House. The girls all sat on one side, the Parents and visitors on the other. When the Sports were over, there was a rush from one side to the other.

On one famous occasion a voice rang out. 'Oh, Mum what a ghastly hat.' After that I warned everyone to admire their Mother's clothes, whatever they thought of them.

Then too, when we had the Chapel we had a lovely Carol Service at Christmas, with the Chapel decorated with delphiniums and lilies. And finally at the end of the year there was the Prize Giving.

The first assistant and I always spent the night before going through all the prizes and cups. On one occasion we did not know that three little boys who lived opposite the school, and usually amused themselves either by getting into bed with me in the early morning or turning the fountain on when the guests had assembled, had wandered into the hall after we had left.

So it was a somewhat hectic Prize Giving with me giving my best glare at the recipient, hissing 'Take it' as the Head Girl received Enid Blyton's *Famous Five*, and the French Prize turned out to be *Make Your Own Clothes*.

Fortunately although some of the girls looked a little surprised none refused their prizes, though there was much interchange afterwards and the Archbishop, who was presenting the prizes looked completely bemused.

'Who chooses the prizes,' he asked. 'Because Chaucer's *Canterbury Tales* does seem a little advanced for a five-year-old, and *Gardening for Children* a little odd for the Head Prefect.'

I hastily explained the girls got prizes they could read when they were older and just hoped he had not seen the face of the Games Captain receiving *Hockey for Beginners*.

Meanwhile the miscreants who had spent a happy evening reading the books the night before had disappeared.

The only other drama at Prize Giving was when the bouquet for me did not turn up, and the Staff rushed round and got some roses for the Distinguished Lady Visitor who on that occasion was taking the Archbishop's place. I wondered what they had found for me and it was hard to keep a straight face when I looked inside the paper and saw a large cabbage, with two roses on the top. I was always glad most English schools did not have Prize Givings, but of course it is episodes like these which made the School such a happy place.

Chapter 21

Archbishop's Housemaid

For a very long time I had been wondering how I could repay the Archbishop and his sister for all their kindness to me. One of the bedrooms at Bishops' Court was set aside for me whenever I wanted it and breakfast in bed was brought up by old Elsie, their faithful retainer. Every Christmas I was invited to join the family party, and well remember how the Archbishop always sent the younger members of the family to run round the garden between courses. It was such a wonderful thing to be part of a family, and it made all the difference to my time in New Zealand.

But in 1952 I particularly refrained from going to stay with them because it was the hundredth anniversary of the founding of the Canterbury Settlement, and I knew they were having many overseas visitors including the Archbishop of Canterbury and Lady Fisher. In 1852 the then Archbishop of Canterbury farewelled the First Four Ships which brought the first settlers to the original settlement. They had to be members of the Church of England; willing to work hard; and have some money to buy land, so that money from the sale could be used to build churches and schools.

It was all arranged that the Fishers would come to Christchurch for the celebrations and stay at Bishops' Court, so that they could join in the celebrations and the Archbishop could preach in the Cathedral. In addition there would be the Archbishops of Sydney and Melbourne, the Bishop of Canberra, and the Bishops of Melanesia and Polynesia. All would be staying at Bishops' Court for several days.

When I looked in to see the Archbishop he was in great distress. 'Oh dear,' he said, 'We are in great trouble. All these people coming to stay and my sister had engaged two people to come and help and now they have written at the last minute to say they cannot come. I cannot think what we can do – send all the guests to a hotel perhaps?'

'Why, Your Grace,' I replied, 'don't let that worry you. I should love to be house parlourmaid to the Archbishop of Canterbury and I am sure your secretary would help too.'

The look of relief on his face made me feel so happy that I could repay a little of his kindness. I rushed off, found the Episcopal Secretary who agreed to help too and all was settled, except we had no idea how to be housemaids. However, we set to work to make all the beds, put flowers in the rooms, and shine up the silver.

The Archbishop and Miss West Watson had to go north to meet the Fishers, so we laid the table and got everything ready. I had prepared a menu in Greek for the Archbishop and we fussed round doing flowers, folding up the table napkins, and putting the finishing touches to the table.

Then the phone rang. The party was delayed so would we please cook the dinner? Everything was ready, and at intervals Miss West Watson rang to tell us what to do.

'Please put the meat in the oven.'

'The pudding should go in now.'

'Have you got the gravy ready.'

We were in a great panic but when Miss West Watson arrived in a great fuss she was pleased that everything looked all right.

The dinner party itself was a great success. We remembered to pass things on the right side, and not to upset the soup in someone's lap. We had borrowed caps and aprons and black dresses and felt we looked very smart. The only bad moment was when the oven door stuck and we thought we might not be able to get the pudding out, but we got it out in the end.

I then had to rush up and turn down all the beds, and do the unpacking and putting away. I met the Archbishop's Chaplain in the passage, holding a beautiful Japanese cope which was to be worn at the service.

'Have you an iron, please?' he asked.

I thought this was tempting providence, so we filled the bath with hot water, and held the cope over it, while the Chaplain told me about the journey out, and how he had to stand guard over the Archbishop and Mrs Fisher as every old lady wanted to sit with them and talk.

All the other Bishops arrived later, and next morning I had to take round the early morning tea trays. I had never expected in my life that I would see a group of Bishops sitting up in bed in their nightshirts. Fortunately the whole party went out to a civic lunch but we had to do an even grander dinner that night as the Governor-General was present, plus other civic dignitaries.

After dinner and washing up, I had to nip out of my cap and apron, change into evening dress and get off to a reception at Government

House. I think the Archbishop was a little surprised to see me there but he gallantly said, 'I think this is the first time, I have drunk champagne with my housemaid.'

I tried to think what else a housemaid was supposed to do. I asked Mrs Fisher, who was not well during the visit, if there was anything I could do for her.

'Perhaps you could do a little washing and ironing?' she asked.

'Why, of course, please give it to me,' I replied.

When I got it I was horrified to see the ironing and washing was Mrs Fisher's evening dresses, and the Archbishop's shirts. What if I scorched her beautiful models which she had brought with her, and I had never ever laundered a man's shirts! However, there is always a first time, and I managed, with a very cool iron to do the dresses.

Then I went off to the Chinese Laundry. 'Please will you wash these shirts as quickly as possible and let me have them back?' I asked.

The Chinaman shook his head. 'Far too busy, can't take any more.'

I argued to the best of my ability. I told him they belonged to the Archbishop of Canterbury, but he was not impressed. I walked out very dejected, and was standing on the pavement when one of the Craighead Parents came past. He stopped and got out of his car.

'You're looking very dejected,' he said.

'So would you be,' I replied, 'if you had a bag of the Archbishop of Canterbury's shirts and no one will wash them.'

'Why don't you try that Chinaman?' he asked.

'I have and he says he's too busy.'

'Here give it to me, and I'll fix him,' he said. Fix it he did to my relief and I was able to put a pile of perfectly laundered shirts on Mrs Fisher's dressing table two days later, to be told I had done them beautifully!

The highlight of the whole visit was the service in the Cathedral and to make it more colourful, everyone who had academic dress was asked to wear it. I finished serving lunch and was rushing to change out of my cap and apron when I nearly collided with the Archbishop.

'I've never seen anyone with so many changes of clothes,' he laughed.

'This is not the end,' I replied, 'I've got a Girl Guide uniform yet.'

All the university graduates lined up for the procession, and I was delighted to find an elderly lady with an Oxford MA Hood who would walk with me. However, our faces fell as we heard the organiser calling out the names of the universities to head the procession. It was, of course, right that the New Zealand graduates should go first, but when we saw McGill, Sydney, Yale and Radcliffe, even Edinburgh and Manchester lined up before us, we were outraged. The final insult was when Cambridge was called and we ended up as the last pair in the procession. As we went along we grumbled that Oxford was founded in the ninth century, and we had been insulted.

'It's an outrage,' fumed my companion. 'I shall send a letter to the Vice-Chancellor in Oxford to say how we have been insulted.'

We arrived at the Cathedral and the organiser gave his final instructions. 'The whole procession will turn round, and the two at the back will lead it in.' To the fanfare of trumpets, Oxford University took its rightful place, and the old lady and I swinging our crimson hoods, led them all in!

It was certainly a wonderful and impressive service and Archbishop Fisher gave a splendid sermon. I could not help thinking of the many immigrants who had come to New Zealand after the war and gone back full of petty criticism; and of the Canterbury Pilgrims, as they were called, who had left everything, and settled with great fortitude in an unknown land.

Back at Bishops' Court I was busy opening the door to all the visitors who wanted to see the Archbishop.

'Can I see the Archbishop, please?'

'I'm sorry he is busy.'

'But I must see him, It's very important.'

Somehow I had to get out of it. They wanted to discuss the Pope, Methodist reunion, Jehovah's Witnesses, and one lady even wanted to read her poems to him. I stood patiently while she read them to me!

The next day we all went down to Lytellton in the morning to see the enactment of the original landing, with the early settlers trudging over the hills to get to Christchurch. Many of the people were wearing the original clothes worn by their grandparents, and kept ever since.

That afternoon there was a huge Mothers' Union gathering, Mrs Fisher was still very unwell but she made a great effort and came to it. I was full of admiration for her courage, as in the morning we had felt she was too ill to make it.

I saw little of this event as I was bending over the sink all afternoon. I had a thousand cups, saucers and plates to wash up but there were a lot of good helpers, so we got them done in good time and packed in their boxes.

By this time I was really rather enjoying being a housemaid and was sorry it was coming to an end. As one Bishop after another departed, I began to feel rather lost, and when the Archbishop and Mrs Fisher were ready to go, I felt very sad. Many people were rather frightened of him, knowing he had been a Headmaster, but he was so kind and charming that he made a lasting impression on the people of New Zealand.

I had already collected a few tips as every good housemaid should, and now the Archbishop thanked me and gave me a signed photo of him which I still have in memory of a very amusing time.

Our own Archbishop had wanted to discuss the question of his retirement, and not very long after this he decided to go and live in Nelson with his sister. I was just as welcome there as in Christchurch, but sadly he did not have a very long retirement.

Chapter 22

Last Days

One of the disadvantages of living in New Zealand before the advent of air travel was that there was nowhere to go for a short trip outside the country, so I was lucky when I was chosen to represent the New Zealand Church Schools at the annual conference of sister schools in Australia. Even so it took four days by sea, and another long coach journey up the east coast to get to Brisbane where the conference was being held.

I found Australia very different from New Zealand. It was fun to see Sydney again but the long journey north was very dull. Used to New Zealand's ever changing scenery, and its beautiful mountains, I found the unchanging scenery with groups of gum trees somewhat depressing. However, Surfer's Paradise outside Brisbane where the conference was held was a very beautiful place with kookaburras to waken us in the morning when we got ready to go surfing before the conference opened.

On the first morning I was surprised to see two ladies surfing in shorts and blouses.

'Is this the regulation surfing outfit?' I asked.

'Oh, no,' they replied, 'you see we are nuns and as it is so hot here, the Pope has given us permission to swim, and the Vatican has designed a special costume for us.'

The conference was most interesting and I enjoyed speaking to the Assembly and meeting the heads of the Australian Schools, some of whom, like the Western Australia ones, had come further than I had. When it was over I decided to visit the Great Barrier Reef and made my way to Hayman Island, from where the boat left.

On arriving at the port I looked round for the steamer and was directed to the smallest boat imaginable. A woman who was waiting had a coil of rope in her hand.

'Do we need rope?' I asked in trepidation.

'It's a very rough journey,' she replied, 'and most people tie themselves to the side of the boat.'

Another woman then appeared. She had had all her teeth out, and lay flat on the bottom of the boat. It was certainly the roughest journey I had ever made, and I spent it clinging to the side of the boat and being seasick. When we got to Hayman Island all three of us had to be carried ashore!

Having recovered I was able to enjoy the fabulous beauties of the Reef. There were expeditions in flat bottomed boats looking down on coral of every possible colour, through the glass hull. Strange sea creatures and tropical fish wandered around. Best of all was wandering along the reef at low tide. It was necessary to wear sea boots as some of the creatures can bite and poison you, but treading carefully we saw all sorts of strange creatures including the big fat *bêche-de-mer*, which are such a delicacy to the Chinese.

The evenings were spent playing Bingo at the hotel, and on my last night I won £75 which enabled me to stay an extra day. Unwilling to face the sea journey again I flew back to Sydney, and on to Canberra, which I found very beautiful with its man-made lake and flowering trees. Friends at the university showed me the magnificent new buildings, and led me up to the great Australian War Memorial.

When I got back from Australia, I thought again what a beautiful country New Zealand was. Indeed while I was there I saw every bit of it, mostly travelling with my friend, Dorothy Govan, Head of Selwyn House School in Christchurch, my little car, and my tent.

We went all over the North Island, staying in Kataia where we helped in the hospital which was short Staffed as the Maori nurses had gone off to a Tangi; and up to Spirit's Bay at the far north. Here, as we lay in the tent on a windy night, we heard the spirits of dead Maoris stopping at the Pohutakawa tree before going off into space.

Like all tourists we stayed at Rotorua, with its geysers and hot springs. We watched the great spurts of water at regular intervals, and felt the constant small earthquakes. In the town you often see saucepans on cracks in the road where the hot springs cook the dinner, or you can wrap an egg in leaves, and hard boil it. This was the only place where we saw the Maoris in full regalia, and we looked at a Maori Pa. Nearby was a modern Maori village with a little church famous for its stained glass window showing Christ walking on the water. Through the figure, the lake outside was a back-ground.

Near Rotorua was Wairaki, where the geysers shot many feet into the air, until the Electricity Board took some of their steam out of them, and Waitomo with its fabulous glow-worm caves which you entered lying in a boat, and keeping quiet in case they put their light out.

Everywhere in New Zealand there are hot pools. We enjoyed those at

Lake Taupo, at Hanmer in the South Island and in Westland.

In the Wairapa I helped prepare bulls for the showring; in Nelson I worked planting tobacco plants; and on the Bay of Islands we helped deliver the cream ration.

One of the most interesting parts of New Zealand was Stewart Island at the southernmost part of the South Island. Here, those who liked to get away from civilisation had settled. One was a Miss Prentice who lived in a small area cut out from the Bush, her only communication with the outside world being the stores delivered at her gate.

'Miss Prentice,' I asked, 'do you not find being cut off from the world like this, a little daunting?'

She paused from introducing all her favourite plants to us.

'Well, yes, my dears, I do,' she said, 'so I have a little hide-out in one of the outer islands where I can go when I want to be alone.'

Because New Zealand is a small country it was almost impossible to get away from school connections. Wherever we went we met Old Girls, past Parents, and relations of pupils. Once when we were walking back from the pictures in a small North Island town we met two present Parents in their best clothes. As we were walking along eating fish and chips out of newspaper, we hastily dropped them down our fronts, with disastrous results!

I also seemed to find long lost relations all over New Zealand. In New Plymouth, while climbing Mount Egmont I met an elderly gentleman who told me of a long ago love affair with one of my cousins, who had rejected him rather than go to live in New Zealand. Another time at the Hermitage, Mount Cook I met two ladies who lived next to some friends of mine in Welwyn Garden City, and most curious of all a family in the North Island who possessed an Oakeley Christening robe, because they had had a remote connection with the family in Victorian times.

So by 1955 I had been all over New Zealand, and I felt my time there was coming to an end. My family had left The Gables, and gone to live in Oxford. Then my Father died and my Mother went back to live in a small house in Eynsham. She was lonely and it was felt that as the only unmarried one in the family I should come back and look after her. My brothers and sister were all married and I longed to be part of a family again, and see their children growing up.

By staying so long I had lost my English superannuation, because at that time you were only allowed to continue for five years when teaching abroad, and Craighead had no pension scheme. After that it lapsed, and at a later date this was to affect my pension, which was smaller in consequence, and forced me to teach on till 65.

I longed, too, to be back in Oxford, and to be able to travel on the Continent; to go to concerts and plays when I wished; and to see all my English friends again. I knew too, if I was to get an English Headship I must go back before I was any older.

Finally, we had a new Archdeacon who was made Chairman of the Governors, and he told me there was to be no more going on leave to England. He thought I should become a New Zealander and remain there.

So at the end of 1955 I gave my notice to the Governors and they began to look for a new Head. This time there was no problem and they appointed Miss Mabel Booth who had been at St Hilda's Oxford, which was my old college. I felt she would do well now the school was established.

I had done all I meant to do. In my last year the chancel had been added to the Chapel and it had been dedicated by the new Archdeacon. There were now 220 girls in the school and a long waiting list for admission; the area had been quadrupled in size with the acquisition of Oakeley, Salmond, and Averill Houses; and the academic standards had risen incredibly. A good Staff, half English and half New Zealanders, was awaiting the new Head, and the buildings were all in good repair.

Nevertheless, it was a terrible wrench to leave. My deep affection for the children, parents and Staff was sincere, and the last few months were saddened by farewells.

The Governors gave me a beautiful silver salver and a diamond and sapphire brooch; the Girl Guides a charming brooch and an Award of Merit; and the Mothers' Union for whom I had often spoken some pearl ear-rings. We had the last service in the chapel which I had built, and loved so well; the last Prize Giving and farewell to parents, Old Girls, and Present Girls who had all given me such support; the last supper with the staff; and the last look at the view of the hills from my bedroom window.

I had come to New Zealand and to Craighead in fear and trembling: I left in a flood of tears as I went down the Craighead drive, along the road to Christchurch; and once again in the boat for England. So I left 'the long land uplifted high' after fifteen years, and wondered what my next venture would be.

LA CHÂTELAINIE

Chapter 23

A Restful Year

I returned to England and ceased to be a Headmistress. It was not, however, to The Gables which my Father had sold before moving into Oxford, but after his death in 1954, when my Mother moved back to Eynsham where she had a small house once occupied by the local dressmaker. She was still very lonely and unhappy and was so pleased to see me home, and planning for me to live with her. It was nice to be back in Eynsham, and to enjoy village life in England again, and for the first few months I was glad to lead a restful life, and enjoy my friends.

However this did not last long. My Mother had a cook and a housekeeper and there was little for me to do, and I began to get restless, and decided to look for something to do.

In April I saw an advertisement in the *Oxford Times* for a temporary teacher of history at the Sacred Heart Convent in Abingdon. They were obviously rather desperate, and I was told one of the nuns would be finishing her history degree in the summer, and they just wanted someone to fill in. I had no difficulty in getting the job, and set off one morning in late April.

When I got there I was taken to the Staff Room by one of the younger members of Staff. 'There are only five lay Staff,' she explained, 'and you're the last to come so here's the broom, get going and sweep the Staff room floor,' which I duly did!

Most of the pupils at the school were Roman Catholics, but there was a smattering of unruly Oxford Protestants, who had failed the eleven plus and were unwilling to go to a modern school. Religious controversy was likely to break out at any moment, until I found my best plan was to arrive early and greet each child as they came in.

'Sit down, get your books out, and have your homework ready,' I said firmly. After the first week I felt I had my class of unruly eleven-year-olds under control, but a message came to tell me to go and see Reverend Mother.

'My dear,' she said in her quiet voice, 'this is a Convent School. We teach by love and kindness. You are being much too harsh.'

'I daresay you do, Reverend Mother,' I replied, 'and they can have love and kindness, now some sort of order has been restored.'

She smiled and dismissed me.

I found it difficult to teach parts of the history syllabus especially the chapters on Henry VIII but I was pleased when the class did respond. One morning the class arrived breathless and full of excitement.

'Miss, Miss, what do you think happened last night?'

'I've no idea,' I answered.

'Battle of Hastings on the telly, just like you said.'

I was glad the television did agree with me!

It was summer and there were many Saints Days, all of which were whole holidays and as the nuns were not allowed to go out, the lay Staff had to take the school on expeditions. We went down the Thames to Windsor, to Warwick Castle, and to London and I always got back pleased because I had not lost anyone! When I went to report to Reverend Mother the nuns were all sitting in a circle in the garden sewing, and it made a charming picture.

Nevertheless the Convent had its sad side. Some of the girls had been left there as infants, because they were illegitimate and unwanted, or the children of actresses who did not want their age known. They never went home like the other boarders, or were visited by their parents. There were also a number of West Indian girls who were quite charming.

The very pleasant term ended all too soon, and I was at a loss as to what to do next. It was impossible to leave my Mother for any length of time as her memory was going and she was liable to do things like turning on the heater when it was beside a chair. There were no suitable Headships or Housemistressships going except in boarding schools. I would have liked to apply for one of these but of course it was impossible to leave my Mother.

I rashly decided to set up as a jobbing gardener, and put an advertisement in the paper. I soon had more work than I could do, and how hard it was! I was paid five shillings and sixpence an hour and most of it was digging weed-covered sections for old ladies who had not had a gardener for years. Most of them watched out of the window to see I did not lean on my spade. But they did invite me in for a cup of Camp Coffee for five minutes, warning me that cleaning the tools was not included in the two hours.

One lady asked me to prune her apple trees and I had no idea how to do it, so I stopped a friend who was passing by and she gave me instructions over the hedge.

It was quite the most exhausting work I had ever done and I got back so exhausted, I was no company for my Mother. I could see the years stretching ahead with me growing more disillusioned and grumpy, so after discussing it with my Mother we decided it would be better if I got a companion for her who would live in, and I would look for another scholastic job.

Idly I looked through *The Times* and *The Times Educational Supplement.* After discarding several advertisements, one caught my eye.

'Experienced teacher required for Swiss School. Must be prepared to live in, and to teach English and History to the English girls. Apply the Head Teacher – La Châtelainie, St Blaise, Neuchâtel, Switzerland.'

It sounded exciting, and a complete change. I wrote off carefully with my testimonials and references, and was very surprised to get a telegram a few days later to say I was engaged, and should arrive on 28th January. A letter followed confirming my appointment, but there was no interview, no phone calls.

I was tremendously excited. I had visited Switzerland in my youth when my father had to pay a yearly visit to an old uncle who lived in a hotel on the Lake of Thun, and the thought of living on the Continent, and learning lots of languages enthralled me.

So off I went to London to buy ski boots, pants and gloves and some warm clothes plus *How to learn French in easy Stages.*

Then the blow fell. Another telegram arrived. 'Regret appointment cancelled. Do not require you after all.'

I was furious, and sat down and wrote to the Headmaster. I thanked him for his telegram and asked him to send me a month's salary in lieu of notice and £50 to cover the cost of extra clothes, which I had had to buy.

Another telegram arrived. 'Come after all. Plans changed again.'

I began to wonder what kind of a school this would be and why there were all these changes. However, I packed up, said goodbye to my Mother and her new companion and set off across Europe.

I had been told a Work Permit was necessary before I could work in Switzerland and I must not arrive at the school without one. So, I got off at Basle Station and after some difficulty found the Health Centre just further down. I was taken into a room, told to undress and shepherded along the passage, without any clothes on, meeting two medical students on the way. They did not seem worried and I went on to have a blood test and X-ray, and then walked back along the passage, thankful to find my clothes again and get dressed. I then received a clean bill of health.

The train went on through marvellous scenery to St Blaise where I got out at the little station and found the Secretary waiting for me. She led me to the village and to my lodging in a Swiss house. My bed-sitting-room was rather curiously situated, as you had to go through the bathroom to get to it, and I saw myself being incarcerated in it every time someone had a bath.

Having deposited my things, I was taken to the Staff room, where I met the other new teacher, Mary Anne.

'What are you going to teach?' I asked.

'English and History to the English girls,' she replied.

'There must be a lot of them,' I responded, 'as I am teaching them too.'

'And,' added Mary Anne, 'I've got a funny bedroom beyond the bathroom.'

'I think,' I added, 'we had better find out how many English girls there are.' We did and there were seven so we thought we ought to go and see the Headmaster.

The charming Swiss Headmaster greeted us warmly, and when the pleasantries were over, I said, 'Headmaster, we seem to have the same job and the same room.'

'Indeed you have,' he replied, 'and it is all your fault,' looking at me. 'You were so unpleasant when I found I could get a less expensive teacher who would suit me better. I was not going to pay you a month's salary or give you £50, so I told you to come. You must decide who has this job. There are always people coming and going here, so the one who does not take this job, can have the next,' and we were dismissed.

Outside Mary Anne burst into tears. 'I've never taught before. I couldn't teach anything else. What a ghastly thing to happen,' she sobbed.

I reassured her. 'You have the job by all means,' I said, 'and I'll have a nice holiday.'

And I did. I was the most popular person on the Staff because I kept offering to do all the unpleasant duties for them: I made up a bridge four and learnt to play it in French; and I took girls hither and thither for appointments which most people found a tiresome chore. In the afternoon I took skiing lessons and pottered about on the nearby slopes.

But after a fortnight my conscience pricked me and I went back to the Headmaster. 'You've been very generous, Headmaster,' I said, 'and I have had a good holiday and enjoyed it, but I can't accept your hospitality any longer. I'll go home at the end of the week.'

There was a pause, then he said, 'Indeed you will not. The Head of the American Department has just given me notice. You will take it over on

Monday.'
   'Very well, Headmaster,' I said, and went off to face my new job.

Chapter 24

Life in a Foreign School

Nothing could have been more different than schools in New Zealand and Switzerland. In New Zealand, heads were urged to proclaim at intervals that the main aim of education was to build character; in Switzerland, international schools were simply there to make money. The fees for the different nationalities varied, the Americans paying most, the Swiss least; and the Staff were paid on the same basis. On pay-day waiters, chambermaids, and teaching Staff all lined up for their pay which was in cash and it was obvious to everyone how much each person got. It was certainly very embarrassing to receive bundles of notes while the kitchen-maid following behind just got two or three. All punishments were fines which went into the school account, three francs for missing lessons, five francs out during the day, ten in the evening.

La Châtlelainie had been a small finishing school run by the Headmaster's Mother, but after the war when American forces came to Europe to live, the school grew to over 400. The Headmaster ran the business side of the school, and spent his spare time hunting in Alsace with his sporting dogs. Sunday night supper was always a nightmare with all the trophies of the chase lining the passage to the dining-room. Everyone was supposed to admire them as they went into supper.

Under the Headmaster was a Headmistress and her assistant and they did individual timetables for each of the 400 girls in the school. Below them were the three Heads of Studies, me of the Anglo-American School, and two others, one for the German section and the other for the Franco-Swiss.

Every morning the twelve French teachers held twelve classes from eight until ten. The other classes did not begin till ten and continued sporadically during the day. The Staff could attend the French classes, which were repeated from two until three, if they wished. The American girls worked for College Boards, the English for O levels, for which few of them were capable.

The Staff Meetings were a *tour de force*. The Headmistress was a wonderful linguist, and switched into five separate languages without any effort.

At the time when I went, the French and Germans were not speaking to each other or sitting at the same table for meals. The usual procedure was:

'Mademoiselle Oakeley, would you please tell Fraulein Schmidt she is on duty this afternoon.'

'Please ask Madame if I could have a new notebook, dear Miss Oakeley!'

Duties on the whole were very light and quite rewarding. Each weekend there were a number of Staff on duty who had to take the girls to the pictures on Sunday; go skiing with them or to local events like regattas or horse shows, or trips on the lake.

One thing which annoyed the English Staff about the weekend duties was that the Swiss and French men never did any. Then one weekend the member of Staff whose duty was to do the list was ill, and I was asked to do it, and of course with a smile on my face I put the men down too.

There was a prickly atmosphere in the Staff room, and one of the French Staff asked if she might speak to me privately.

'You cannot do this, Mlle Oakeley,' she said when we were alone in one of the top classrooms. 'You do not understand.'

'Why not?' I asked.

'You do not understand our customs.'

'Perhaps you would explain them to me,' I hazarded.

'Do you know how expensive Mistresses are in Switzerland? On the salary the men get in this school they could not afford such luxuries, so they must cross the border into France at the weekend. So there is no time for them to do supervision duties.'

The list had to be changed!

In the Anglo-American department there were twenty-five teachers under me, most of them Americans. Most of the Staff at the school had a good reason for being there. Some were Frenchmen who were avoiding their military service; a number of the men were homosexuals who could not get jobs in boys' schools; some of the English Staff had had problems with discipline or drinking; and the Russian master who did a sideline selling swim-suits to the Staff had been turned out by the Communists, while the elderly Spanish teacher had been forced to leave Spain, because of his opposition to General Franco.

Most curious of all was the Bursar, an elderly German who doled out our money, ruled the Science Department, and was constantly asking us to play bridge. We were all rather afraid of him and I was very surprised when one day, looking out of the Staff room window, I saw him talking to the Headmaster, and looking very uncomfortable.

'Why he's actually afraid of the Headmaster,' I exclaimed.

'Do you wonder,' said one of the French Staff,' he was in charge of one of the big concentration camps in Germany in the war, and at any time the Headmaster can turn him over to the authorities.'

I found the American Staff in my department were very rigid teachers. The Latin teacher came with his notes on every lesson for the year, and he used them every year without changing them. I taught English which meant using a series of books full of stories of the man who was dreadfully injured but ran in the Olympic Games etc. When I started teaching Shakespeare the girls were delighted.

One of the advantages of teaching in Switzerland was that there was an easy solution to all Staff problems. Opposite the School was a little *estaminet*, and when anyone was in trouble I used to say, 'Well never mind. Let's go over and have a brandy and tell me all about it.'

It was here in the little *estaminet* we often had Staff parties in the evening. I can still remember one Burns night when we taught everyone how to dance a reel, some of them on the tables, and the French secretary who had a great affection for the British Royal Family, finding a kilt she had brought from Edinburgh, and whirling it round in great style.

After I left Mary Anne's room with its accompanying bathroom, I went to live with a charming Madame Schimdt, who had a house called Soldoré on a hill looking over the lake. I had a lovely big room with a small wash-room attached, but no bathroom so when I wanted a bath I had to go down to the school. For some obscure reason which I never understood, the school telephone was in the bathroom and just when one was having a good soak, the phone would ring, and a voice would say, '*Monsieur est là?*' and you had to get out, wrap yourself in a towel and go out into the passage to fetch the secretary.

It was to Madame Schimdt's house that we eventually moved our parties. Since my room was so large it was ideal and we used it to celebrate every possible occasion from Swiss Independence Day to the Queen's Birthday. We had glasses of Beaujolais, and Swiss canapés which everyone enjoyed. For a time we had a play-reading society which was most popular, and the local Swiss joined in with us.

Among the Staff was a young Frenchman called Luc who was extremely amorous and kept a book with the names of all the Staff who had slept with him. It was often shown to a select few and there was always rejoicing among the French when a new entry was made.

It was after one of the parties that Luc hovered behind to help clear up.

I managed to get some of the English Staff to stay behind too, but it was obvious Luc was going to wait until the very end.

When they had gone, he went through the door and then turned and said.

'*Mary, veux tu me baiser?*'

'Certainly,' I replied and gave him a smacking kiss on the cheek, and showed him out. It was not until long afterwards that I discovered *baiser* did not always mean to kiss!

By now I had become friends with Mary Anne who was teaching for a year before getting married. Unlike me she had not had her medical on Basle Station but in Neuchatel itself. To her horror, when the result came through she was sent for by the Headmaster, who told her it said she had syphilis and would have to leave at once.

Naturally she was in a terrible state and we did not seem able to get any help in the school, so for two days she sat in my room, wondering what to do.

'The only thing to do,' I suggested 'is to go to a Swiss doctor privately, and see what he says.'

'But how can they have found it?' she asked. 'And how can I get married if I've picked it up somewhere.'

However, after two days we got an appointment with a Swiss doctor who took another blood test and found it was negative. He then got in touch with the Swiss Health Authority and found they had mixed up the blood tests, and Mary Anne's had been negative all along. Her father who was a Medical Officer of Health in the north of England was very angry over the whole episode, and protested to the Swiss authorities about their mistake.

This was not the only time I had to soothe Mary Anne. One day she received a phone message to ring her fiancé urgently that evening and she spent the day in great agitation. 'I can't imagine what has happened,' she said miserably.

'It's probably nothing serious,' I said.

All the same I was relieved when she got through that evening and came back looking very happy.

'What was it all about?' I asked anxiously.

'It was just to tell me he loved me,' she replied.

Chapter 25

The Students

Just as New Zealand and Swiss schools differed from each other so the girls at the Châtelainie were quite different from the New Zealanders. Apart from the seven English girls, all those in the Anglo-American School were Americans who had done part of their education at schools all over the States. As each state has its own system of education, it was very difficult to teach subjects like English grammar, because those from some states might not have learnt any, while others had done it for years. The girls from the east and California were well ahead of those in the mid-west.

I was fully aware of the differences the first morning. While New Zealanders had to be pushed along, and later I was to find English girls standing rigidly at attention, the Americans were bright and friendly and quite unorganised.

'Oh, Ma'am, what a pretty sweater.' 'Ma'am, I do like your hair-do.' 'Ma'am, I saw you in the French classes. Do you like them?' were some of the opening remarks which greeted me when I met the class. Of course I had to reciprocate, by admiring their dresses, their hair, and their jewellery.

The older girls, particularly, were very keen to learn because they wanted to go on to the Ivy League Colleges in the States and for this they needed College Boards. When I begun teaching Shakespeare there was great enthusiasm because most of them had not met Shakespeare's plays before.

One of the younger girls cabled back to her Mother in the States, 'Momma, I'm learning Shakespeare.'

And once when I was tackling *St Joan*, someone else cabled, 'Momma, I'm reading a play by George Bernard Shaw.'

Most of the older girls had regular boyfriends, some of whom lived surreptitiously in St Blaise or Neuchâtel, and were visited on the quiet. This was a usual excuse for missing lessons, but I was astonished one day when three girls were missing one afternoon.

'Where are they?' I asked, and then added rather facetiously, 'I suppose they have gone to get married.'

There was a pause, and then someone said, 'Well, as a matter of fact, Jeannette has.'

'And,' I added, 'I suppose the other two are bridesmaids.' It turned out they were.

Jeannette had lived in Paris, and had a boyfriend unacceptable to her parents, so they sent her away to school in Switzerland. The boyfriend followed, and they put up the notice of marriage on the church door, past which staff went every day. After a certain time, under Swiss law they could get married.

I had to go down and report this. The Parents were summoned and the Headmistress investigated, as the Headmaster was abroad, in the States. At first there were great recriminations but by the evening all had calmed down, and the Parents gave a wedding party at the local hotel to which we were all invited.

The girls slept in houses all over the village. At night the duty Staff had to escort them down, and lock them in. In the morning the maids went in, unlocked the doors and saw the girls off to school. On snowy or cold mornings they just looked up and said, '*Malade*' and went to sleep again until the school nurse came to rout them out.

One evening when I was calling the roll in the hall of one of the houses, the door banged shut. As it could only be opened from outside I was locked in. It looked as if I would have to spend the night when one of the girls said; 'Would you like us to knot some sheets, Ma'am, and let you down?'

This did not appeal to me.

'Or we could show you a nice little path over the leads and down that way.'

Nor did I wish to do that!

There was another long pause, and then someone said, 'Well, Ma'am, we might as well tell you. We had a key made in the village long ago.'

I must say I did not blame them as in case of fire they would have been completely trapped.

The highlight of the year at the Châtelainie was the tour to Italy. Escorted by the Headmistress and some of the French Staff, the girls went off to Florence, Rome and Venice staying in the best hotels, and being escorted round all the famous buildings. For this they liked to have all new clothes, either made by the Swiss dressmakers in the village, or sent from Paris.

However, in my second year, the night before the tour left the

Headmaster sent for me and said that as there were so many American girls going to Italy he would like me to go too, with the Headmistress, one of the French Staff and a house matron. I was thrilled, and we set off next day, crossing over the Alps into Italy and arriving in Florence. We stayed in a luxury hotel where your clothes disappeared overnight, and arrived all washed and pressed next morning. At each meal the Head Waiter brought the staff some special delicacy as a tribute from the manager, no doubt hoping for the return of the party next year.

From there we went on to Rome. It was quite an ordeal escorting some sixty beautiful girls through the streets, with young Italians calling 'Beddo' hopefully as they ran beside us. Some accosted the teachers asking if they could come to the hotel to enrol their sisters at the school!

I was, however, rather taken aback when the Headmistress told me that the foreign girls and the three foreign teachers were going to one hotel, and the American and English girls were to go to another with me.

'And, Mlle Oakeley, you must be sure they do not go out at night,' remarked the Headmistress.

So Mlle Oakeley saw the girls to their rooms and then went down and tipped the Night Porter, and told him to ring her if a anyone went out from then on.

The second night I was happily reading my Continental *Daily Mail* in bed when the phone rang. 'Mlle, it is the Night Porter speaking at twenty-two-fifteen. Two of your young ladies have just left the hotel.'

Throwing on my dressing gown I rushed downstairs (to the astonishment of those sitting in the foyer) but it was too late and I went back and dressed. I then went into the nearest bedroom and asked if anyone knew anything about it.

'I expect they have gone to the Fountain of Trevi,' the girls said. 'They wanted to see it by moonlight, you remember and you said they could not go, because the male escort was at the other hotel.'

Off I went to the Fountain of Trevi but they were not there and by the time I got back to the hotel I had a bevy of young men following me and shouting 'Beddo, beddo' very cheerfully.

When I got back I sat down to think. The first thing was to find out who was missing, and I got a passkey from the porter and set off to find out.

Unfortunately I had forgotten that two of the American girls had not liked their room, and they had had to be moved to another. So when I opened the door of one room I found an astonished looking couple in bed, who stared as I said, 'Pardon,' and rushed out!

After I had checked everyone, I discovered it was two English girls aged sixteen who were missing. While shopping in the afternoon, the American girls told me, they had met two Italian journalists, and had gone to a night club with them.

I asked the American girls if they would have gone out with them.

'Why, no, Ma'am,' they replied. 'Not with a couple of unknown pick ups. If it had been those American boys we met in the bar here, it might have been different!'

It was only then I remembered I was not in overall charge of the party and rang the Headmistress in the other hotel. She came at once and took charge.

'It is no good,' she told me, 'there are at least thirty night clubs in Rome. It is useless to think of looking for them. We must just sit and wait till they come back.'

So we did and sat in the lounge drinking coffee while the Headmistress told me horrifying stories of what happened to girls who went out with unknown young men at night. By 7am we were both half asleep, when the two girls walked in.

The Headmistress rushed up to them. 'Tell me, tell me at once, did they profit of you?' she asked.

But they did not understand what she meant! 'We've been out with two young men, and had a very good time,' they replied. 'What's wrong with that?'

'If you don't know, I'll tell you later,' I said.

By this time they were rushed upstairs and locked in their room while the Headmistress rang the Headmaster in Switzerland. He immediately dispatched one of his Staff to fetch them back, and on their arrival cabled their Parents and sent them straight back to England. Their Parents were furious and complained that it was a very trivial offence.

The episode, however, was not over. The next day we left for Venice and as we were sitting in the train waiting to go, the two young men turned up with huge bunches of flowers. They were politely told that the girls were ill and had gone home but they did not believe it. They then got on their motor bikes and followed us to Venice, breaking into the dining-room, as we were having our evening meal. They were still holding their flowers, which were drooping. Again they were told the girls had gone home.

Upstairs, saying goodnight the girls were full of discussion.

'Do you really think they have gone, or will they come up and assault us?' somebody asked.

Looking at the girls with their faces covered in cream and their hair in curlers, I did not think it likely.

From there the tour was peaceful, gliding about in gondolas and eating ice creams in St Mark's Square, we were able to enjoy Venice without any more incidents.

Later I had to take the American girls to Geneva to do their College Boards, but they were no trouble and we had a most enjoyable time.

Chapter 26

Variations

Next to New Zealand, I have loved Switzerland more than any other country. At La Châtelainie we had to work only on weekend in three, and the rest of the time were able to do what we liked. In the winter it was skiing, though I never got really good; in spring it was walking among the flowers which came up everywhere when the snow melted; and in summer it was driving off over the great passes like the Furkil and the Grimsel, or idling away time on the lakes. I was fortunate to have my car there, and was able to take other Staff into France for the ski jumping; off to Einsildehn to see the wonderful Abbey; or over to the Jungfrau to go up the incredible mountain railway to Jungfraujoch. Each Friday I had a group of Staff of all nationalities asking me to take them with me.

One of the best trips was to the Val d'Iser, the last place where nomads lived as they migrated down to their fields in the winter. I had three American Staff with me, and the road up to it was somewhat perilous. We started back late and had got to Martigny when one of the girls found she had left her valuable camera at the top of the pass, and I had to drive back in the dark to get it. The American men thought I should not have gone, and there was a tense atmosphere until we got safely down.

Another occasion we went up the Great St Bernard, admired the dogs, talked to the monks, and slept *en masse* on a communal mattress on the floor!

But perhaps the best of all was going up to Gstaad where the school had an annexe. Once, Monsieur drove me up as I had to supervise the American staff there, and on the way he told me all the history of the area, and how the Counts of Gruyère terrified all the surrounding countryside.

It was at Gstaad that I remember how I was trying to teach a class who were simply not listening. Finally I looked up at the balcony of the house next door, and saw the handsome young Aga Khan sunbathing, and realised what was the distraction!

Once I had to hurry to Gstaad where one of my Staff was threatened by dismissal. She had been put in charge of one of the chalets and two days later the Headmaster saw a photo in the paper of two of his students at one of the night clubs with two young men at two o'clock in the morning. He showed her the magazine and asked her what she thought he paid her for, and as a result she could go home to England the following week. It took all my persuasion to make him change his mind!

This was not the only problem I had to face with the Staff. One of the older men came to see me and asked, 'What are you going to do about Julian?'

I thought the problem was that he was drinking too much, which was a common problem among the staff, but it turned out he was a homosexual. All went well until we had a dance with a local boys' school and then the other men had to lock him in his room as he was so frantic. He had once been a pretty golden haired boy; had then been assaulted at his public school; and then settled down with a companion at the university. Eventually he had tried to make a break and thought he might do it by coming to teach in a girls' school.

So we set up a system of 'surveillance' by which someone in the department kept him company every night, in an effort to keep him away from the public conveniences in Neuchâtel. We felt we were getting somewhere when he got a letter from England, from the friend with whom he had lived, saying he was coming to St Blaise.

'It was to get away from him and start a new life that I came here,' wailed Julian. 'You must all help me to get rid of him.'

After a conference it was decided to write and say Julian had gone to teach in France and was not at St Blaise any more. In order to make it official I 'borrowed' some of the Headmaster's notepaper, officially headed, and one of the men wrote the letter.

We were a little surprised when the Headmaster came storming into the studio.

'Who's been stealing my notepaper, and forging my name,' he roared. And to me, 'Did you write this letter and forge my name?'

'Certainly not, Headmaster,' I replied.

'And you,' he shouted at the other master. 'Did you steal my notepaper?'

'Why no, Headmaster, I would not dare,' was the answer.

The Headmaster went away furious, and we discovered the recipient had thought the letter somewhat fishy and sent it to the Headmaster. So we had to make other plans.

When the man turned up at the local hotel, the Cheval Blanc, we persuaded Julian to go in and say he did not want to see him. Three of us waited outside saying he had just five minutes. Fortunately he did come back, having told his erstwhile friend it was all over and he had better go home. The tears were streaming down his cheeks so we bore him off for the inevitable brandy.

Next morning one of the men went down to the Cheval Blanc pretending to be a plain clothes detective and told the man to get out of Switzerland at once or he would be arrested, and he went.

This was not the only problem. One of the Staff got badly into debt and was put in the Swiss debtors prison where we were interested to visit her. She was then extradited to France and we had a farewell party on the border, together with the Swiss and French police. Later a letter came to the Staff saying she was in the La Fresne prison where she was chained and could we club together to get her out. The sum was too large, but one of her old French teachers paid up and all was well.

By the end of the second summer term I was beginning to think I could not stay at La Châtelainie for ever, and started applying for headships in England. At first I did not have any luck.

I got into the last two in the first school and was then taken aside and told, 'Well, Miss Oakeley, you have not got it, and you will know why. The other candidate was a Housemistress at this school; has had experience at another girls' Public School, and so has had a perfectly ordinary teaching career. And you – teaching all over the world, that is what lost you the post.'

So I tried again, this time for a northern school. Again I got into the last two and the governors could not make up their minds. Finally they chose a northerner as being more suitable for a Merseyside school, though she only stayed a short time, whereas I was twenty years in my next job!

On the way back, my escort asked me if I was in for any other job, and when I said, 'No,' asked me if I had applied for St Felix, Southwold.

'Is that going?' I asked. 'If so, I will apply.'

I had spent many happy holidays in Southwold when a child as my grandmother had had a house there in summer, so I applied and asked the Headmaster if I could go to England for an interview.

'Twenty-four hours only,' he said flatly. 'You've been away too much.'

So I flew from Zurich to London, and found myself walking along in the city where the last interview was to be held. As I got near a man rushed out of a doorway, and knocked me over. My stockings were ripped, and my skirt covered in mud. I threw myself on the mercy of the Commissionaire at the door, who kindly sponged my skirt.

'You'll have to take your stockings off, Miss,' he said.

So I did and waited with the other candidate for the interview.

I entered in some trepidation. Fortunately, the other candidate had gone in first so I had time to compose myself. I put my bare legs under the table with some relief, and hoped no one noticed the dark patches on my skirt. Most of the questions were about my time in New Zealand, and at the end I was offered the post and accepted it. In actual fact I did not see the school and had only a vague remembrance from my childhood.

Then I had to get back to St Blaise. I rushed to London Airport only to find it was closed owing to fog. After a wait we were put on a bus to catch a boat, and went via Dunkirk to Paris. I had an airline ticket from Paris to Geneva, but could not cash it in and had to go by train. Unfortunately I had not enough money for the train ticket, but by a stroke of luck I met an airman who was off for a skiing holiday in Switzerland. It was a time when foreign exchange was very limited and with great daring I persuaded him to pay for my ticket on a promise to pay him back when we got to Geneva. He kindly obliged, and stuck to me like a leech. On arrival at Geneva we went to the bank together, and I paid him back and he was delighted with all the Swiss currency.

At Geneva I got a train to St Blaise, ran all the way from the station, and arrived at 10am just in time for morning school. The Headmaster was in his study and I hurried in.

'I heard on the radio, there was heavy fog in London,' he said, and added, 'I did not think you would make it.'

'Headmaster,' I replied, 'you said be back within twenty-four hours, and I have succeeded in doing it, though it was a bit of a rush. At lunchtime I shall be coming to give you my notice as I have been appointed Headmistress of St Felix School, Southwold, Suffolk, England.'

In April I paid a preliminary visit to St Felix, driving down from Eynsham to Southwold. Leaving the main road, I caught sight of a huge mass of red buildings, and as I got nearer I was appalled. If New Zealand and Switzerland had been in complete contrast St Felix was different again. There seemed so many buildings, so much land on both sides of the road, and I could not see how I could possibly manage it all. How foolish not to have viewed the school before I accepted the Headship! My heart failed me as I came to the entrance, and I fled down into Southwold whose Vicar had once held a mission in Eynsham. Unfortunately he was out, so after having a quick brandy in the Swan Hotel, I returned to face the music.

Then it was back to La Châtelainie for the summer term. Switzerland was looking its most beautiful with its mountains and flowers, and it was hard to say goodbye. We made a last farewell visit to Eiselden with its lovely abbey; gazed on the Jungfrau and the Lake of Thun; and had fondu parties with the staff in Neuchâtel. All too soon the Headmaster told me he had found my successor and I was to initiate her into the work.

This was the only occasion in my life that I met someone who was totally evil. In fact I could not believe such a person could exist. She took Julian the homosexual out and landed him outside the men's lavatories in Neuchatel; delighted in helping the alcoholics to get drunk; mocked at the play reading and affronted the Swiss by jeering at their English accents; and ran me down in front of the students. Fortunately the Headmaster saw my point when I reported all this, and cancelled her appointment.

So I left La Châtelainie, and my many friends. Later I was to hear of its sad ending, with the Headmaster, heavily in debt, saying goodbye to his staff, and shooting himself among his dogs in his van. The elderly lady who had controlled the Staff died soon afterwards and the school closed down.

ST FELIX

Chapter 27

A Different School

On a preliminary visit to St Felix it was snowing hard, and a cruel east wind was sweeping over the playing fields. At the main entrance I met old Mrs Young, surrounded by a host of black cats. She had been the Founder's maid, and told me I was the fifth headmistress she had welcomed. She and her husband, who was the caretaker lived in two small rooms all among the class rooms at the school. When they were due to retire the Governors asked me to inquire if they had enough money for their retirement bungalow, and Mrs Young proudly showed me a trunk in the corner of their sitting-room full of notes which they had put aside from their wages over the years!

Even at forty-three I felt too young and inexperienced for the job and this feeling deepened when I met my predecessor, Dr Williamson, a famous Headmistress and a brilliant scholar. I spent three days with her and each day added to my feeling of inadequacy and anxiety. We went through lists of highly qualified and experienced Staff; met the Bursar, Commander Egerton who managed house, grounds and finances; toured the five houses and vast sanatorium; and looked at the honours boards full of successes at the universities.

The school had been founded in 1897 by Miss Isabella Gardiner, daughter of Samuel Rawson Gardiner, the Cambridge historian.

'I want to found a school for sensible girls,' she had said. 'One where there are few rules, no prizes or rewards; very little uniform, and no gates or fences so that anyone who does not like it can walk out.'

She was very serious minded, entirely occupied with founding the perfect school and continued until 1908 when she had a very serious breakdown and eventually had to give up and live a quiet retired life on the south coast.

'Did Miss Gardiner ever come back to see the school she had founded?' I asked Dr Williamson.

'Yes,' she answered,' she did. She had to live a very quiet life after she retired, but she used to come back in the late evening, wander round her school in the moonlight, and depart before the girls were up next day.'

The second Head was quite different. Miss Silcox was very artistic, the friend of John Masefield, and the buyer of many beautiful things for the school. I always thought she had a marvellous death, listening to her favourite music in her friend's house on Boars Hill.

Number three was Miss Edgehill who was a great builder, and added many important buildings, and number four was, of course, Dr Williamson who had a most difficult time managing the evacuation of the school to Dorset.

The comparison between St Felix and Craighead was astonishing. Instead of a bedroom among the dormitories I had the most beautiful house with four bedrooms, three bathrooms, a large drawing-room opening onto the garden, and a large and well kept garden. Instead of one building into which everyone was crammed there were five separate houses all purpose built. St Felix was one of the few public schools in England which was built as a school, not as in so many cases starting with a large private house.

Instead of the constant search for Staff both teaching and domestic, they were all there – a highly qualified teaching Staff, and a large domestic Staff. There was also a large maintenance Staff, who did all the carpentry and plumbing, and a host of gardeners. It was wonderful, when the plumbing packed up at the weekend, just to dial the workshop, and someone came up at once and put it right.

There were large and extensive playing fields, too, at St Felix. Two lacrosse pitches, three hockey pitches, hard tennis courts, and a beautiful swimming pool. My mind went back to the thrill when we acquired a piece of land for a not quite full size hockey field in New Zealand.

St Felix was, of course, managed by a Governing Body which met mainly in London. It consisted of University dons, business men, sometime parents and Old Girls, only meeting once a term.

At the first meeting one of the Governors took me aside and said, 'Now look, we don't want you bringing up all those little things. We have engaged you to run the school, and just go ahead, and only bring the big things to us.'

Again I had memories of the monthly meetings at Craighead, held in the evening with a lavish supper in the middle. Every little thing from the buying of a new set of saucepans had to be brought up but the big things waited until after supper when the Governors were well fed!

Then there was a beautiful Chapel at St Felix given by one of the parents, complete with a lovely picture by the anonymous Von Lucca. It had everything a chapel needs, and there had never been any struggle either to build it or to furnish it.

There was too, of course, great contrast over the girls, so different from the Americans with their lovely clothes and neat hair styles, or the New Zealanders full of bounce and go, eager to do anything that came to hand. The St Felix girls wore Aertex shirts, shorts, grey socks, and sandals, in which the younger ones looked very sensible and neat but the older ones, particularly the Sixth Form, looked terrible. For best it was a green silk dress and a white shawl, scrabbled round the shoulders. Camel-hair coats were the best part of the uniform, but were topped by brown felt 'pudding' hats, crammed down over their eyes.

Used to the gay chatter of the New Zealanders, and the witty conversation of the Americans, I found it very difficult to get near the English girls. The older ones mumbled and looked at their feet; the younger ones simply fled when I approached. Conversation at meals was agony with a flat 'Yes' or 'No' in answer to every effort on my part. Their manners were impeccable as they said 'Good morning, Miss Oakeley', when I met them on my way to school, but otherwise they avoided me.

There was also a deep contrast with the Parents. Because Craighead was so small and the parents all knew each other, the beginning of term was always extremely cheerful. Parents all dropped in to see me, bringing jars of cream or dumping legs of lamb in the kitchen. If anything was wrong I dealt with it, as it was my fault, whereas at St Felix I got complaints about things in the houses which were not my fault. The American parents I never saw at all, and at St Felix they mainly went to the houses, and only serious complaints came to me or went straight to the governors.

Work was all important at St Felix. There was an Entrance Examination, the Common Entrance for Schools, and a girl had to have an IQ of at least 112 to be accepted. The only relaxation was organised games; hockey and lacrosse in winter; cricket and tennis in summer. Apart from Sunday walks to church the girls seldom left the grounds, and because the school was isolated, and the parents lived a good way off, there were very few outings.

One of the advantages of Craighead had been the proximity of the local hospital, which was only a few streets away. Although St Felix had a large sanatorium, complete with cook, housemaid and two nursing sisters, the hospitals in Norwich or Ipswich were an hour's drive away even by fast ambulance. Fortunately we had two excellent school Doctors one of whom attended every day but every sick girl seemed to have an extended convalescence when I first went to St Felix, and some lost a lot of school time when being escorted for walks after illness by the nursing staff.

So there were many advantages in my going to St Felix. When at Craighead, I knew nothing I could do would make it any worse: at St Felix I knew one false move might wreck it!

It took me some time to get used to the isolation of the Headmistress. On my first day, I put on my best dress and waited for the Parents to come, but they all went to the houses and only one elderly retired Housemistress, complete with calling cards visited me. At outing weekends, I always felt very out of things when I saw all the parents loading up their cars and fetching their girls, and I waited in case one came to make a complaint.

Then at Craighead my word was law. I decided what everyone should do, where we should go for outings, when they should wear their summer uniform. At St Felix all this was done by the Housemistresses, and I had to wait for the weekly Housemistresses meetings for any decisions to be made.

Usually at these I put forward suggestions and the reply was: 'But it has never been done,' which was rather frustrating.

I well remember the first time there was to be a whole holiday and I asked for suggestions as to what the girls would do, having in mind that I would send them down to the beach for a picnic. There was a deadly silence, and then someone said, 'But they always practise cricket on a whole holiday, ready for the house matches.'

There is much to be said for the system of Housemistresses because it gives the girls individual attention, in a small group; there is someone to turn to in trouble; and there is a healthy and happy rivalry between houses. In the early days of girls' Public Schools, it was an ideal system, because each competent Head of Department waited for the day when the Head would summon her, and ask her to take over a house. But as the years went by, the senior Staff preferred to buy houses in Southwold, or they were married, or had elderly relatives to look after, or simply wanted their weekends free. So the applicants for housemistress posts were often divorced women who found it difficult to get on with the other Staff; or younger ones who were often not responsible enough; or kindly people who could not keep order.

But the main difference between the two schools was the climate. How I missed the New Zealand sunshine, the clear blue frosty winter days, and the lack of rain to prevent functions! I often thought of it as I stood on the playing fields watching matches in a bitter east wind or when the old

Russian teacher said, 'It's just like Irkutsk. It's just like Irkutsk,' as she met me on the way to breakfast.

No one would wish all schools to be alike, and it was a challenge to become Head of a school so different from the previous one. Now I was to have leisure to play my part in the community; to join in conferences and meetings with other Heads; to enjoy entertaining people in my beautiful house, where excellent meals could be served; and to learn how to organise and run a much bigger school. All the previous Heads had been at the Universities of London or Cambridge and it was a complete change for St Felix to have a new Head with an Oxford Degree, experience overseas, and a background of small private schools.

Chapter 28

First Impressions

Before officially taking over at St Felix on 1 August Mother and I stayed at the Swan Hotel while the house was re-decorated. But I had no furniture and no money, though the Governors kindly gave me a loan to buy furniture, I had an elderly housekeeper called Violet who was deeply suspicious of me but we soon became great friends and I was very fortunate to have her to look after me.

With the end of the holidays came the ordeal of going up to St Felix to meet the Staff. I dreaded my first Staff meeting as I had not met any of them and I was always grateful to one of the Music Mistresses, who escorted me in to the library where they were all sitting. It was a very formidable array, and my mind went back to the entire Staff of Craighead, five in all, sitting round a table.

So to the next day when the girls arrived, and the day after when I walked into the Gardiner Hall, clad in my gown, and stood on the platform gazing at the full assembly of St Felix School.

I told them how as a young girl I had always wanted to go to St Felix but my Father said it was too far; how when I went for my Oxford interview at Lady Margaret Hall, there was a girl from St Felix; and how this was the end of a dream to find myself standing on the platform.

Then they all went to their classes, and I went down to my office to do the letters with my two secretaries, to see my most able deputy and the nursing sister, and when that was over to go and teach.

This was one of the best things about St Felix. Not only could I teach my own subject, and the years of it I liked, but I could choose my class, have what books I liked for them, and be unsupervised. So I chose the two bottom classes, the first intake aged eleven plus, and I taught them ancient history. When in my first class I asked who had liked history at their previous schools, most of them said it had been very boring, and I set out to remedy that. It was certainly lovely to have my own history room, and to be able to fill the shelves with exciting books.

The best contact I had with the girls was the Morning Assemblies, and

I feel it is sad so many schools have given them up. Here one could pass on complaints, talk about interesting things, get them to know the Bible from the readings, and pray for any cause or person for which they asked.

In the evening there was a service in the Chapel which was optional. I was surprised it was so well attended until I found out the Housemistresses chose ten girls for each service, and sent them. As the years went by this was given up and we concentrated on the Sunday services. There was always a good choir and bit by bit the girls were allowed to take part and we brought in local clergy to preach and help out our Chaplain, who at first was also the vicar of Reydon Church. Confirmation took place every year, and almost everyone was confirmed, though St Felix was not a Church School and was one of the few girls' public schools which took Jewish girls as boarders.

As there were so many beautiful churches in the neighbourhood I often took the girls to one of them on Sunday. It was a pleasant walk to Blythburgh or Walberswick; or we went to the lovely restored church at Great Yarmouth, and picnicked on the beach afterwards; or just went down to the lovely Southwold Church when Southwold Jack rang the bell to start the service.

I had decided that I would not make any changes in my first two years. My first task was to learn all the girls' names. Each day the secretary handed me a school photo and I asked her, 'Who's this? What is the name of the tall girl at the back? Is that one Elizabeth's sister?'

In the end it took me three weeks to learn them all, and later I was to be very shocked when visiting a school run by one of my ex-Staff where she had been Head for six months, to find she only knew half her girls.

Nevertheless there was one change the governors had instructed me to do as soon as was possible. When the school came back from evacuation there was no building suitable for the juniors. Originally they had been at Centre Cliff in Southwold, but this had been sold, so they went into Bronte House which was one of the senior houses usually.

This was a most unsuitable arrangement because the children had to work at the senior school, and had to go backwards and forwards, and the top junior form was divided, half being in Bronte and the rest in the senior houses. There were few fully trained Staff for teaching juniors, and the senior Staff were not qualified to teach them. They also had little privacy – whenever they were out in the grounds they were either ignored or petted by the seniors.

The other problem was the Sanatorium, which for weeks at a time was unoccupied and so was very expensive to run. Colds and minor ailments were dealt with in the houses, and it was only when there was an epidemic that the San was really useful. Modern treatments and antibiotics had decreased the length of time the girls were in bed in the San.

So it seemed a sensible thing to put the juniors in the old San and build a new small San on the end of Bronte.

Like all changes it was hotly opposed, not by the St George's staff and children who were delighted. New classrooms were added, and as the bedrooms were all small they were more suitable for younger children. Three classes were organised with three primary trained teachers, and their own Staff for music and art, though they still had to come down to the senior school for gym and music and swimming.

But, of course it was a blow for the Sanatorium Staff, who were moved down to a pleasant small San of twelve beds, with only daily Staff, and having to have their meals in school, when the San was empty.

If there was an epidemic, Bronte House was cleared, and could be run from the San.

The Old Girls, who in most schools are opposed to change, objected to the San moving but were delighted at the re-opening of Bronte House. When the juniors were there, it had two long dormitories only, but these

Laying the foundation stone of new buildings at St Felix

were now cut up into small rooms, and as the house had a separate dining-room, this was an added bonus.

Those from the other houses who volunteered to move to Bronte went for various reasons. Some could not get on with their Housemistresses; others had Mothers who were Bronte Old Girls; while a few thought it was an exciting new experiment.

After St George's moved, it got many more day girls, and by sharing a coach from Lowestoft with the local boys' school it increased its day girls, and Bronte, with between forty and fifty girls increased the numbers at St Felix. I was quite determined the school must be bigger (it was about 210) and could only have a reasonable Sixth Form if it grew bigger. This was opposed by the Old Felicians who thought I was ruining the school, but as the years went by small private schools all over the country closed, because they could not offer a complete range of subjects.

One other change had to be made, too, as I really could not bear the school uniform. So a competition was held for a new design and all the artists got busy. Finally it was decided to abandon the navy blue which had crept in, and go back to the green which had been the original school colour. Velvet dresses replaced the green silk and shawls; green pinafore dresses took the place of Aertex blouses and shorts; and gold jerseys, and green blazers were added. On the whole the school looked much smarter.

By the end of 1959 these changes were complete and I was happy that on the whole they had gone smoothly – the numbers had increased substantially.

Chapter 29

Extra-Curriculum Activities

With its splendid buildings, and devoted Staff, St Felix was able to offer many out of school activities. From the earliest days it had been a very musical school and a large music block of practice rooms and orchestra room had been built. There were two school orchestras, and a House Musical Competition judged by some famous outside person! There were music teachers to cover all possible instruments: and a music scholarship to bring in able pupils.

Every term there were three concerts which the whole school attended, and many famous people came to the school. One of them was Julian Bream to play his lute, and since it was a long way to come, he spent the night at my house. While he was dressing I heard a cry of agony: 'I have not brought my studs. My housekeeper must have forgotten them when she packed my case. Can you do something?'

I realised the only buttons I had were pink and blue and so unsuitable.

'There's nothing for it but to sew you in,' I called, and sew him in I did, suffering agonies during the concert in case the stitches gave way!

Most popular of all the performers was James Blades on 'The Instruments of the Percussion'. The girls liked him because he was responsible for the banging of the gong in films. A more controversial performer was Bruno Hoffman, who brought a dinner waggon of glasses of different sizes. When he moved his fingers round the ones with the top notes, some of the girls found them too shrill and had to go out. Gerald Moore, talking about accompanying, and Evelyn Rothwell with her oboe were other performers.

And of course, there was the Aldeburgh Festival to which the girls loved to go, especially when it was *Noah's Fludde*. Occasionally a top Continental orchestra came and the tickets were not all sold. Then the Box Office would ask me to send the Sixth Form to fill the empty seats, provided they wore mufti!

Art was another favourite at St Felix and a beautiful new art room was built on the top of the old labs. The art Staff had Monday off, and were in their room all the weekend. Scenery for the plays; attractive pottery; and every kind of painting was enjoyed.

In addition there were clubs covering most subjects – photography, classics, pets, cercle Francais, Astronomy, Science, Play Reading, Social Service, Guides, Jazz, Stamps all had clubs run by Staff, often at the weekends.

Other clubs took the girls further afield. Riding in Lowestoft, sailing on the river by Blythburgh, fencing and golf were all enjoyed.

But perhaps the most popular extra-curricular activity was dancing at the boys' schools. This was suggested to me soon after I arrived at St Felix. 'We're invited every term, and the invitation is always refused,' lamented the Prefects.

I put the idea to the Housemistresses.

'It would be very difficult to supervise that the dresses were not too low,' said one.

'You're not suggesting they go in their green silks?' I asked.

'I suppose we should have to stay up to give them warm milk when they got back?' asked another.

I pointed out I did not think their Mothers performed this service when they went to dances at home.

'But who would take them? I certainly do not feel it is my responsibility,' moaned another.

'I will,' I replied.

So the invitation was accepted, and accompanied by the Sixth Form we made the long journey to Felsted, where I had a very pleasant evening with the Headmaster and his wife, and we all got back safely.

This was just the beginning. By the end of my time at St Felix there were four dances a term, including one for the Upper Fives, and everyone enjoyed them, including the younger members of Staff who took over from me.

The next development was trips abroad, and they were popular too. The Games Staff enthusiastically took parties skiing; the French Staff organised trips to Paris, to improve the French; and the Geography Staff arranged parties to go on a cruise to the Baltic and the Soviet Union. Unfortunately, because St Felix pupils did not all come from wealthy homes, not all girls could join in, but some worked in the holidays or persuaded their grandparents to help, and usually managed one of the trips.

Social service had always been a great feature of St Felix, and each house gave an entertainment per term to raise money for their own particular charity. The school also had a social service cause for each term, and assisted with local charities.

One of the social services activities was the yearly party for the people of Bulcamp Home for the elderly, which was near Southwold. In the early days many of the inhabitants were mentally ill, and I well remember when all the visitors were old men, who came without an attendant or nurse, and I spent the afternoon assisting them to go to the lavatory. Such are the duties of a Headmistress!

The outstanding events for the social service representatives was a journey to Southwark Cathedral to present purses and afterwards to meet Princess Margaret in the Goldsmith's Hall. Each school was represented by its Head Prefect, and there had been much colloquy about what to wear. However, when the girls were all lined up, Princess Margaret, who was enjoying a post service cigarette, had not been told she was supposed to speak to them and started to leave.

Seeing the disappointed look on all the faces of the Head Girls, I boldly went up to her and said, 'Your Royal Highness, I think the girls want to meet you,' and she graciously turned back and saved the situation.

But the most important of the social services activities was the New Guinea Mission. One of the Old Felicians, Olive Blake who had been in New Guinea with her husband, Peter Robin came to tell us about her work there. We often had a Sunday evening talk about some charity and their work, and this was one of the most interesting.

Instead of asking for money, Olive suggested we built a school in New Guinea where there were very few in the Highlands. After some discussion the Prefects organised a Working Day in Southwold and Reydon and raised the £250 necessary to build the first class room.

'My sister and I were given the task of cleaning literally hundreds of prayer books in Southwold Church.'

'We spent the afternoon turning out and cleaning a whole lot of flower containers, followed by a delicious tea.'

'We were shown a garage and had to clean two bicycles.'

The Old Felicians raised money to equip the school, and the Chapel Guild gave money from its funds. We also had Father Bodger, from the New Guinea Mission, to tell us about the country and its people which he knew well. However, like all efforts to raise money the cost rose steadily and we had to raise another £700 before the school could be built. We eventually got the full amount and it was handed over to the Bishop who visited the school in 1965.

The school was built of light materials because of the climate, and it was for boys only, which rather surprised us. It did not take long to build and soon we had photos of the boys and the class rooms, and even a letter from the Australian Headmaster. We sent out a St Felix Flag, identical to the one which flew over St Felix on important occasions, and sets of books marked St Felix School.

Olive Blake went back to her work as a nurse in the baby clinic in the Highlands but eventually came back to live in Norwich and so could keep in touch with us. Later one of the Old Felicians, Daphne Shillitoe, who was doing voluntary overseas work was able to visit the school and give a first hand account of it.

Not only were there were many extra-curricular activities at the school but I was able to pursue some of my own. While I was in New Zealand I had been made a Lay Reader in the Anglican Church, the second woman lay reader to be chosen, and I had gone all over Canterbury preaching and taking services. The one I remembered best was a Women's Service in the Baptist Church, which turned out to be a women's service for men, and the sermon had to be changed hastily!

When I first came to St Felix women were still not allowed to be Readers, but eventually the Anglican Church in England gave way, and again I was the second woman to be appointed. It made it much easier for taking services in the Chapel, except that I still had to ring round trying to find someone to celebrate on Sundays when the chaplain was not available.

It was certainly interesting going round the Suffolk churches, many of which were sadly falling into disrepair, or had to share a vicar with several other parishes. I remember going to one large church to take the Sunday Mattins, and there were four people present, three women and one man.

'Do you want to leave anything out?' I asked hopefully, thinking perhaps the Magnificat, or the second set of prayers might be left out.

The answer was: 'We may be few, Miss, but we love the Lord, and don't want to miss anything on a Sunday.'

So we went through everything, and as they could not sing nor could I, we had to say it all.

At St Felix I had a day off on a Wednesday which was delightful. The housekeeper brought up breakfast to me in bed, and as soon as the school had gone to Assembly, I got in the car and went off for the day. Until 1968, when my Mother died, I often had to drive the 172 miles to Oxford, there and back to see her. I came back one night in blinding snow, arriving at 1am and when I rang up next day to know how she was, her companion said, 'She was just asking when you were coming'!

But other times I went to Norwich to the splendid library, or the Maddermarket Theatre, or just to shop, or I visited my many friends in the neighbourhood, and came back refreshed and exhausted, just hoping some awful tragedy had not happened in my absence.

Chapter 30

Half Way

By 1968 I had completed ten years at St Felix. I think one of the things I enjoyed best was interviewing both girls and Parents. Each year there were large numbers of 11-year-olds for Common Entrance from preparatory schools and state primaries. I always liked to interview those who were at all possible, and found it most entertaining. In addition there were the State Bursars who had all their fees and uniform paid. Possible candidates and their Parents arrived in Lowestoft or Norwich, and all had to be interviewed by the Heads of the three Suffolk schools.

Once I interviewed a small girl and asked her why she wanted to go away to board at St Felix.

She replied, 'I don't, but me Mum thinks it would be to my Social Advantage.'

Needless to say I let her go to one of the big day schools.

The State Bursars who were chosen by me for their intelligence since we were a very academic school, were a great asset. It also helped to make a social mix with Parents coming to functions in their Bentleys and BMWs and others getting off the bus.

It did sometimes make problems as when one State Bursar came for advice, 'I don't know what to do about Mary Anne,' she said. 'You see, she asked me to stay, and there was a butler, and meals in a grand dining-room. How can I ask her back to eat in our kitchen?'

'Why did you enjoy your visit so much?' I asked.

She answered quickly, 'Because it was different.'

So I responded, 'And don't you think for the same reason Mary Anne would enjoy meals in the kitchen?' And she did.

But the State Bursars were often at a disadvantage when it came to leaving school.

I was once talking to a very able girl who was trying for Oxford Entrance. 'You really must try to make some conversation when you go for your interview,' I advised, as I tried to prepare her.

'I can't,' she said flatly.

'But you must think beforehand and have it ready,' I suggested.

'You don't understand,' she said sadly. 'My Mother runs a working men's hostel in Liverpool, and in the holidays I act as a housemaid, I never hear any conversation which would help me get to Oxford.'

One of the things I enjoyed at St Felix was taking people who were prospective Parents round the school. Many schools left it to the girls, but I enjoyed meeting people, and showing off the many things the school had to offer.

Once when I was showing a Mother and daughter round we came to the chapel, and they fell on their knees before the altar.

'Now, Amy, get on your knees and pray to God that Miss Oakeley will take you into her nice school,' was the remark. Of course after that I had to take her!

During these first ten years there were many alterations to be made and of course it was hard to find the money, as St Felix had no endowments or outside properties. First we tried an Appeal, but it raised only £59,000 and offended many of the Old Felicians; then much against their opposition we let the school in the summer holidays, which enabled me to put proper central heating into all the houses, which had had open fires up till then. Eventually we managed to sell our gravel in the part of the school grounds opposite the playing fields and this not only gave us a good income but extra money for scholarships.

Armed with this extra money, two more improvements were made in these years. A new general Science laboratory and Biology room, an art and craft department, were built on the top of the old laboratories, and the old Biology lab became a Geography Room. This was a very popular move.

But the worst arrangements I found at St Felix were those of the dining-rooms. Each house had originally fed in its own house, but on return from evacuation the Housemistress' sitting-rooms in Gardiner and Somerville had to be sacrificed as dining-rooms for Clough and Fawcett. The kitchens, meant only for one house were far too small and contained little modern equipment, and when we had the end of term supper we were served with cold meats, and jelly and ice cream.

So the grand plan for the dining-rooms was made. There were to be five, one for each house, plus a Staff dining-room, all grouped round a central kitchen. They were located next to Clough and Fawcett Houses, and Bronte was to abandon its own dining-room (which Parents and girls objected to very strongly), and joined in with the others.

Every modern improvement like dishwashers, was included and a catering company took over. No longer would the Lady Caterer come to me imploring me to find her some Staff or a frantic search begin for a new cook, all was now in the caterer's hands.

Nevertheless all did not go smoothly at first. Although the food was incredibly better, the girls were getting more exciting and different meals at home now, and they expected more lavish meals in the new dining-rooms. The domestic Staff who had never gone home till after 10pm because it took so long to wash up by hand, found their wages cut and retaliated by putting bits of broken china in the washing up machine and breaking it. In actual fact the new dining-rooms were one of the most successful and much needed changes at St Felix.

In all schools about this time the Sixth Forms were beginning to get restive. Already boys' schools were taking Sixth Form boarders, largely because they were short, and Sixth Formers were more mature and grown up. Gradually the large dormitories were cut up into small rooms, until all the Upper Sixth had small study bedrooms to themselves, but this was not enough. So when a large house called White Gables came up for sale, the Governors decided to buy it, and make it into a Sixth Form house as an experiment. It was not very far from the school, and the Upper Sixth duly moved in, and were delighted by the change.

But it was a failure. It divided them off from the school, and they spent all their time down there, ignoring lectures and concerts, hardly going out at all, but sitting in their rooms Playing their transistors. The neighbours continually complained about the noise, and boys besieged the house at night, so I had to think of a better solution.

Changes too had to be made in the organisation of the Prefect system. The Prefects chosen by me and the Staff were an elite group. They had special privileges, such as more outings, and were very unpopular with the rest of the Sixth Form. The Prefects worked in their second year, and a major disaster occurred when one of the best of all the Head Girls failed her A levels. So in 1968 the prefects were abolished and replaced by a School Council, which was made up of all the Lower Sixth who took office, plus the Head Girl in their second term. This left the Upper Sixth two terms free of duties to do their revision, and about the same time they gave up wearing uniform.

The school council included those who maintained the discipline; those who liked doing jobs like the locking up, and everyone had a job of some sort. On the whole it worked well.

A minor improvement during these years was a proper car park and exit road, which saved me from furious Parents at weekends who got their cars scratched.

Meanwhile I was enjoying my beautiful house. I had my own bedroom and bathroom *en suite*, and the two spare rooms, one with all the New Zealand pictures, and the other with the Swiss ones and a bathroom in between, plus the housekeeper's room and her bathroom.

I inherited Dr Williamson's maid, Violet who was in her sixties and a real character. She had been an orphan child, and had been trained in a nearby convent, and then moved to St Felix where she was very happy.

We certainly had some episodes together. She objected that I had not as many beautiful things as my predecessor. One of the complaints was the lack of fish knives and forks. When my rather grand cousin came to stay, Violet produced fish and chips just to shame me, but fortunately when I was telling this story at a dinner party, the guests said they had a spare set, and the omission was rectified.

On another occasion after I had had the Sixth Form for coffee on a Sunday night one of them put her used anti-histamine holder in an odd bucket she saw by the back door. Next morning Violet put the hot coals from the fire in it, and I was awakened by a terrific blast, and rushed down to find Violet had lost her eyebrows.

For dinner parties, of which there were many, food could be brought over from the kitchen, and extra help came in to wash up. Later, in retirement, faced with my own cooking nervously prepared, and mounds of washing up when the guests had gone, I thought how lucky I had been at St Felix.

All this time my Mother was much on my conscience. I had to find a companion and a housekeeper who would stay, which they seldom did, and just at the most awkward moment a telephone call from Eynsham would tell me they had walked out. By the time I went to St Felix, my Mother's mind had quite gone, and she could not be left. I found the only way to keep the Staff was by sending them off in the holidays and taking over. This meant I could never leave my Mother.

One August, I had just received the O level results and my Mother had gone to rest upstairs. I was so absorbed that I did not hear her come down and go in the garden, until I heard her scream and found her with a broken hip on the garden path. The local doctor, a locum at the baby clinic, was two hours in coming as my Mother lay on the garden path covered with a rug. Eventually the ambulance was summoned and we rushed off to Oxford. But neither the Acland Home nor the Radcliffe Infirmary could take her, and we ended up at the Nuffield Orthopaedic at 11pm. It was a terrifying episode for my Mother who had not been out of her house for many years.

In April 1968, I was exhausted with looking after her, and felt it was not fair to St Felix to go back at the beginning of term so worn out. So, when the companion and cook housekeeper came back, I decided to go up to my cousins in Nottingham for the last weekend.

When I arrived the phone was ringing and it was the local doctor to say my Mother had just died and would I come back at once.

Tired as I was, I turned round and started off home. On the way I passed the battlefield of Naseby, and a sudden thought struck me, 'Now I am free, and can go back to New Zealand to see how everyone is, how the school is faring (not too well I feared) and revel in the glorious sunshine during the summer holidays.

Thus ended my first ten years.

Chapter 31

New Zealand Again

At the end of July 1968 I went back to New Zealand. This time I flew, but the plane made many stops on the way. Frankfurt, Athens, Bahrain, Bangkok and finally Sydney after a long and tiring flight. However, there on the airport was Margaret, once gym mistress at Craighead, and now married to a Sydney business man. My visit with her was short, but I thought Sydney was looking as beautiful as ever with the gums and yellow wattle in flower. We walked along the beach, and once again saw the beautiful harbour, the great Sydney Bridge and the Opera House.

And so back to New Zealand, and the first sight of the 'great land uplifted high' of Abel Tasman. But as we neared New Zealand I began to have doubts about coming. Would anyone remember me? Would the whole visit to which I had looked forward so much be a failure? Would the new Head of Craighead resent my coming?

When we reached Christchurch there was a delay as there was a VIP on board who had to get off first. We all waited and then the Air Hostess came to me and said, 'Could you please get off, as everyone is waiting?' Off I went and there was a crowd of Craighead Old Girls with bunches of flowers all waiting to greet me!

A further hold-up occurred in the Customs as there was a Foot and Mouth outbreak in England, and the New Zealand farmers were afraid of people bringing it into the country. We all had our shoes dipped in disinfectant, and they smelt awful for the whole of the trip.

From then on it was one long whirl of activities. The first was a splendid buffet dinner for all the Christchurch Old Girls. It was followed by other great reunions in Timaru, Dunedin, Nelson, Auckland and Wellington. I was given beautiful presents, a book of views of New Zealand, a lovely sheepskin rug, some Maori knives. It was quite difficult to remember everyone's names but I managed!

Apart from all the happy big reunions there were various highlights of the visit. One was a visit to Blue Cliffs where I was able to ride again, though I had got to the stage where I needed a mounting block! It was lovely to see all the New Zealand Bush again.

I chose the opportunity to get my friend Helen to drive me down to the Haast Pass, where we had once walked the track with great adventures. By this time the road had gone through, and we were able to go through at a leisurely pace, exclaiming with horror when we saw the remains of the dirty huts where we had stayed. We saw the Franz Josef and Fox Glaciers again and the little church with a plate glass window looking out onto the Franz.

So back to Christchurch and along the beautiful Kaikoura Coast to Nelson where Miss West Watson was now living. I was sad that the Archbishop had died, but glad to see my old kind friend again. To greet me she lit an enormous fire in my bedroom and I could hardly sleep for the heat, but it was a kind thought.

Also in Nelson was my old friend, Marion Cocks Johnston who was running a farm there. She and her friend had a hard life growing vegetables and flowers for the Wellington Market. One morning we picked beans, which was a back breaking job; Marion then took them into Nelson to sell; but as there were no buyers she brought them back and we had to bury them.

After Nelson I left the South Island and visited my old friends in New Plymouth. We tried to climb Mount Egmont but met a party coming down carrying a dead girl who had been killed by falling stones and we went no further. So, on up to Auckland to catch the overseas plane.

The only part of the trip I had not enjoyed very much was visiting Craighead. As I had expected the Head was not very welcoming but she did agree to my attending a service in the Chapel, which was what I wanted most, and nothing else mattered.

There was a slight hold-up in Auckland, which enabled me to be taken round to see all its beauties. Sitting on a peninsula between two harbours Auckland is one of the loveliest cities in the world.

It is always cheaper to fly round the world rather than go backwards and forwards the same way, so I had arranged to stop in Fiji on the way back as I had an introduction to some friends there. Suva really was the loveliest island, and I enjoyed every minute of it – seeing the gorgeous flowers, the smoke-blue mountains, and the men on the outrigger canoes. My friends took me all over the islands, and I thoroughly enjoyed my visit.

When it came to catching the plane to go home, I had to leave early as the Fijian pilots could fly only in daylight, so we arrived at the International Airport at Nandi at 6 pm. The Air Hostess pointed out there was a very nice hotel near the airport where we could get dinner, and wait until the international plane went at midnight, so off we set.

As we walked along we met two lovely looking Fijian girls in their best dresses and flowers in their hair. Coming up to me they said, 'Would you like to go to a wedding?'

I was a bit taken aback but enquired where was it?

'Oh, just up the road,' they replied, so rashly I left the party and jumped in the taxi with them. But it was not 'just up the road'. The taxi started off uphill, along a winding road, getting deeper and deeper into the mountains.

I got quite alarmed, and when we saw an American airman walking along I asked, 'Do you think we could pick up that airman, please? I should feel much safer it there was a man about.' They agreed so we stopped and picked him up and eventually arrived at the village where the wedding was taking place.

The wedding was attended by men only and was presided over by the Chief in all his glory. A tremendous feast was laid out in long trenches and we were introduced to the Kava Ceremony. I had read in the *Reader's Digest* that when it was offered you drank it in one gulp which I did but the taste was terrible. After that we ate sucking pig and many strange fruits. Then we were taken to the long houses to meet the women and children who were having a feast of their own.

Later, we went back and the bridal couple sat with the Chief while the men sang and danced. Finally the Chief came up to where I was sitting with the American airman and asked, 'Have you enjoyed the wedding?'

'Oh, yes, yes,' we replied.

'And did you like the dancing and singing?'

'Very much, thank you.'

'And now it is your turn to entertain the company.'

We were horrified. The American airman turned to me and asked, 'Ma'am, can you sing?'

'Not a note,' I answered.

'Then I guess we'll have to dance,' he said hopefully. We went through all the dances we knew and finally decided on the Palais Glide. Everyone was lined up and we careered round the arena.

As I wheeled round clutching a large fat Fijian naked to the waist I wondered what the staff and girls of St Felix School would think if they could see their Headmistress now!

Like Cinderella I suddenly realised it was getting late and I had to catch a plane so the Chief was summoned, thanked and asked to get a taxi. I kissed the Airman and the two girls goodbye and set off in a taxi driven by a most murderous looking Indian, and with many waves of farewell we hurried down the mountain. I feared I should never reach civilisation again, and was much relieved when I saw the control tower of Nandi Airport.

The other passengers were sitting waiting.

'We've had a boring evening sitting in that hotel,' they said, and asked, 'what have you been doing?'

'I've been to a wedding,' I said, 'But I don't think anyone believed me.

So we climbed on the plane, crossed the Date Line sometime in the night and arrived in San Francisco at 6 pm.

'We've booked you all in at a hotel again,' called the Air Hostess.

'Are you going to spend your one night in San Francisco in bed in a hotel?' I asked the lady next to me.

'Certainly not,' she said. So we looked around and found a Yellow Cab who agreed to take us if we could find three more people. With some difficulty we persuaded two businessmen who were drinking in the bar to join the party, and finally found a foreign lady who did not speak any English.

'You would like to see San Francisco?' I hazarded, but she did not understand.

I took her by the arm and showed her the taxi, but at that moment the Air Hostess came up.

'What are you doing with the woman?' she asked. 'She is in my charge, and must stay with me.'

'She wants to see San Francisco, by night,' we answered. 'We'll look after her,' and we pushed her into the Yellow Cab and told her to say 'I go, goodbye,' to the Air Hostess who shook her head.

While the rest of the passengers slept in their hotel, we toured San Francisco, stopping to gaze at the Golden Gate, and the famous bridge; looking at the Spanish Galleons moored by the Harbour; and gazing at the huge area of China Town, and the lifts to get up and down the hills. We had drinks in a cafe full of soldiers off to Vietnam, and got back just before midnight, to see a relieved Air Hostess retrieve her charge.

I fell asleep on the plane, had a glimpse of Kennedy Airport, and by early morning we were in England coming down at London Airport. I phoned St Felix, and was back there ready for the new term after a wonderful holiday.

ST FELIX

2

Chapter 32

Back in Harness

I had thought a good deal about future plans for St Felix while I was away overseas. There had been significant changes in my first ten years. In 1958 there were 210 girls and by 1968 there were over 400. For a time we had had two boys in the Sixth Form, but it was not a popular move. One of them later got a Cambridge Half-Blue, and worked for the National Front. When I first went to St Felix it had been entirely female, and most of the girls had crushes on each other or the Staff. Then gradually male Staff were appointed, and by the end of my time at St Felix Sunday afternoon was the occasion when Cambridge undergraduate callers were being entertained in the houses.

There were still three building projects I had to complete. The entrance to the school was through the cloisters which had also been given in the early days. They were one storey and when I proposed building on the top, there was further outcry. However, the Governors were in favour and a Geography Room, two Maths Rooms and a Language Laboratory were built on the top. The maths rooms were divided by a partition which could be pulled back and the rooms used for examinations which had always caused problems when the Gardiner Hall was used for them.

Then there was the problem of White Gables which we eventually sold and built Nightingale House near the main buildings, in the school grounds. It had all single rooms for the Upper Sixth, and they could have some meals down there and they were delighted.

Finally there was the swimming pool, built in the early days. When I first brought over an Australian PE mistress she told me the girls were the fastest swimmers she had ever seen. She changed her ideas when she measured the pool which was only 23 metres instead of 25. This made it useless for competitions, so it had to be taken to pieces, lengthened and a diving pool built at one end. About the same time The Parents gave the school two squash courts.

We tried to make life easier for the parents, too. The original outing plans when Parents came down to Southwold hotels and took their daughters and their friends out proved too expensive, so for exeats we ran coaches to London and Cambridge, and Parents were encouraged to bring caravans and camp on the playing fields if they wished.

As in all schools Parents were most generous and co-operative. Over the years Parents Meetings and a Parents Association began and were most helpful.

At first I had found Parents Day at the end of the summer the most difficult of all functions to organise. Since the Founder would not allow a Prize Giving, which was an easy way out I had to think of something else.

The first Parents Meeting was terrible. I gave a report and then the Parents were encouraged to ask questions such as, Why aren't the girls allowed to wear lipstick? Why can't they have more outings . . . go to bed later . . . work in the school library until late . . . go for walks etc?

All these questions were devised by the girls who asked their Parents to ask them on their behalf. As the school grew larger the Gardiner Hall was too small for gatherings of Parents and they had to go outside. Fortunately for me we never had one wet occasion in all the years I was at St Felix.

So the Parents Days had to be replanned, and I went back to the Craighead idea of entertainment. At first we just had dancing or PE on the playing fields; then we had a different entertainment in each house; and eventually we had Pageants with the whole school.

The entertainments began in a small way. There was a lovely garden called The Sunken Garden, given by the Old Felicians, and here we did a small pageant on the Wanderings of Odysseus. Again we were fortunate in all the Staff who helped with enthusiasm, the Classics Mistress being most enthusiastic.

The next idea was to perform *Comus* one evening in the cloisters. It was unfortunately the coldest night of the year, but the Parents mostly had hot toddies to revive them. This was a great success, and I then decided to do something bigger.

It was rather an undertaking to write and produce a pageant for over 400 girls, getting the costumes, and properties and hoping for a fine day. Fortunately the Staff liked the idea and helped me to make it a great success.

The first pageant was 'The Queens of England' based on *The Histories* written by Agnes Strickland who had lived in Southwold and was buried in the churchyard. Parts were written for girls with special talents, and each form did a scene.

We began with Boadicea who had such a connection with East Anglia.

I chose a girl with red hair who was supposed to be a competent rider to take the part but she turned out to be very nervous and when the horse drawing her chariot nearly bolted she was almost thrown. However, a brave and experienced horsewoman seized the bridle and all was well.

We got Mathilda safely out of Oxford Castle which was always in danger of blowing down, and saw a procession of elegant French Queens, before meeting Queen Elizabeth talking to Shakespeare. Finally we saw Albert and Victoria at the Braemar Games when tossing the caber came in for much amusement.

We were fortunate to have a number of foreign girls who came after their term was finished and since most of the medieval Queens of England were either Spanish or French they loved acting the parts. On one occasion Catherine, wife of Henry V did not appear at the right time and I found the foreign girls all sitting under a tree.

'You should be with the others waiting to go on,' I called to them.

'But our complexions. We cannot sit in the sun or they will be ruined,' they wailed.

From there we went on to do a pageant of the History of the School with Miss Gardiner and her Father looking for a site, and on to a History of the United States starting with Columbus. Here we had great trouble with the covered waggon on its way to the west, but the Indians enjoyed attacking it. Every pageant had some animals in it. But after the donkeys in one pageant ran off to Walberswick Marshes in the morning and had to be rescued by Lower Fifth, the Biology Master who was in charge refused to co-operate any more. Two final pageants made the set complete.

The Parents enjoyed the pageants because everyone likes to see their own child in action; the Staff did too, on the whole; and the girls loved them.

But it was not only on Parents Day that we went in for pageants. When the Anniversary of St Edmund's Martyrdom came round, Southwold asked us if we could do a play about St Edmund. This, of course, was a grand way of teaching history and I took the juniors over to Hoxon where St Edmund was murdered under the bridge, so that they could get the feel of it.

The play was called 'The Arrows of the Crown'. There were some spectacular fights with the Danes all round Southwold Church and in spite of it being a freezing cold night everyone survived including me who was doing the commentary, and the Whippet who was representing King Edmund's greyhound. To use the proper entrances it was necessary to go outside and I came upon a touching scene of the Church Wardens wiping the performers' feet!

From this first play in the church we went on to produce a nativity play in Southwold Church each Christmas. There was a beautiful rood screen in Southwold Church and it made a perfect setting for the angels. For some years we had a lovely girl with long fair hair, and she made an Angel Gabriel framed against the arch. Southwold Church was in the gift of the Simeon Trust which was very Low Church and we had to be careful not to offend them. On one occasion we had to make the Wise Men abandon their censers and have their frankincense in boxes!

Once during the year each house put on an entertainment. Sometimes there were parties in the houses and Fawcett House loved to have a Hallowe'en Party for everyone.

One year Clough had a party with all the school in their house enjoying it. I was late and as I left the phone rang. 'Did you know,' a growling voice said, 'that I have put a bomb in Clough House. It will go off at six-thirty.'

I raced across to Clough House, seized the Fire Bell and rang it loudly much to everyone's annoyance. They all went outside, much to the fury of the Housemistress who wanted to know what on earth I was doing.

Everyone was duly accounted for, and at six-forty went back into the house, and I went back to mine with a sense of relief that nothing had happened.

Each year there was either a House Music Competition or a House Drama Competition. Unfortunately, there always seemed to be one house who either had no musical people or no one would could act so when I was allotting houses after Common Entrance I tried to remedy this.

Then there were the expeditions to places all over England and the Continent. To Norwich, Yarmouth, Cambridge and Stratford, and to Paris or Brittany and to Switzerland or Austria for the skiing.

The expedition I enjoyed most was when I took Lower Fourth on a history expedition to Burgh Castle. We had done the Roman Occupation of Britain in history. It was at Burgh Castle that St Felix met St Fursey and they decided St Felix should preach Christianity to the East Angles, and St Fursey should make his way to France, to see what he could do with the French.

After Burgh Castle we went to Fritton Church where there was a window dedicated to St Felix and a three-tier pulpit. The expedition ended with a row on Fritton Lake which was the highlight of the day.

So life was not all work at St Felix though it was an important part, and examination results were a very important part of the school year. Yet many Old Felicians have told me how much they enjoyed the music, the drama and the expeditions, and I could safely say life was never dull. In a number of boarding schools the only activity at the weekends is watching television, and I always felt a full life was a happy one.

Chapter 33

Iran

In the 1960s foreign girls began coming over in large numbers to English schools, mainly in the Sixth Forms. Most of them came from Singapore, Malaysia and Hong Kong. They certainly found the work in the Sixth Forms difficult because they were used to having their work supplemented by tutors, and found it difficult to think for themselves.

Among the girls who came was a charming girl, Soussan from Iran and she invited me to go and stay with her Parents in the holidays.

I had already been to Iran because two New Zealand friends were doing a science project in the schools there. I spent a few days with them in Tehran where I found the traffic quite terrifying. We found one whole street which was given up to repairing cars. It was the time of the Shah and we saw his fantastic jewels in one of the Banks and his lovely palace whose gardens were open to all.

After a few days we set off south and saw all the fabulous places of ancient times, like the tomb of Cyrus the Great at Pasargadae; the sacred city of Qum; and the beautiful Maidan at Isfahan. This is the city of beautiful bridges, where people picnicked in the arches. There was an English church there, and we went to Communion where the bread was a huge mat, from which we tore off pieces.

So on to the city of Shiraz, going under the arch of the Koran. It is the city of roses, the city of the poets; and was the most beautiful one we saw in Iran.

Next morning as we were having breakfast, a large man came up and said he was driving out to see the nomads moving out of their winter quarters, and turning to the man of the party asked him if he would like to go.

'Can we come too?' I asked.

He replied, 'Sorry, far too rough going for women,' and off the two of them went to get ready, but when they got to the car there were the three women in the back seat, and he could not get us out.

The Nomads had wintered in the south, and were moving off to wander through the Middle East in the summer. They carried all their possessions. Some were on camels, others on horses; nets on the horses contained either cats or hens. Somewhere I had encountered it all before, and of course it was the story of Abraham's migration in the Bible.

Next day came the visit to Persepolis, the great city of Darius, destroyed by Alexander the Great, some said to please his mistress. Here we saw wonderful carvings of Persian soldiers, coming to pay tribute; the remains of the palaces and the great rock carvings. On the way back we saw the tombs of the Persian Kings, with a strange square building adjacent, whose purpose has never been decided.

From there we went to Isfahan again to look at the fabulous mosques, and gradually made our way back to Tehran.

Yet amid all this splendour, one could not help noticing the poverty. As we drove through the deserts a woman was waiting with a baby and a toddler holding out her hands for food. There was no provision for widows or orphans and we felt they would die in the desert. In a restaurant a woman was drinking a bowl of soup and giving sips to her baby.

'Is that all she has?' I asked the waiter.

'It's all she has all day,' he answered.

Yet the Shah was spending huge sums of money on the great archway near the airport, which was to welcome visitors to Tehran; more again on his Coronation; and finally over a million on the festivities at Persepolis.

I wanted to go to the Caspian which I had often drawn on maps but it was not possible, and anyway I had seen many beautiful cities and mosques, and could look back on a very happy visit.

On the way back from Iran I visited my niece in Qatar. This is in one of the rich oil states and was full of contrasts. Great palaces and mosques being built, and yet camels wandering about in the main street. The new prosperity comes from oil, and everywhere we saw the great derricks, and saw the oil men at work. The heat was appalling and I decided I would not like to live there.

Then in 1976 I paid my second visit to Iran, a completely different one from the first. On this occasion I stayed with the Mossanen family. Dr Mossanen was a Jewish dentist and they lived in a beautiful house on the outskirts of Tehran. I began badly as I had brought some whisky not knowing they were all teetotallers! We also sat gazing at the food at the first meal as I did not know the visitor must help herself first.

The walls of the house were covered in lovely Persian carpets, and there was a permanent guard outside all the time, because there had been many attacks on Jewish people in Tehran. Indeed one night when we went to visit one of the Grandmothers (which we did every day) we could not get in as the answering phone was out of order. A crowd quickly gathered shouting 'Dirty Jews', and I was thankful when the gate was manually opened.

The two girls in the family were not allowed out alone. The elder one was at an all woman university; the younger one, Soussan, at St Felix. They asked me if I would like to go to tea at the Hilton, and when we got there asked me to excuse them for a minute. Quite soon several young men appeared, who had been telephoned to come and we had an interesting party!

One thing I wanted to do was to go shopping with Madame, but she did not seem to want to take me. Eventually she said she would and we set off. A small boy with a basket on his head was hired to carry everything.

'Does he not go to school?' I asked. 'I thought you had compulsory education?'

'Yes, we do,' replied Madame, 'but many must earn money to keep their families.'

When we got back, I thanked Madame, and she replied, 'I enjoyed it too. You see I had never done it before, as the servants always do it.'

Another day I went out with Dr Mossanen, and he took me to see the Secret Police Headquarters. We went into a room where there were little piles of clothes waiting for the relatives to collect. The owners had either committed suicide or been executed. Then Dr Mossanen asked me if I would like to go into an adjoining room and look at the bodies, but I refused. He told me he was responsible for shipping back to the States the bodies of Americans who died while in Iran.

One day Dr and Madame Mossanen told me they were going to take me to a matchmaking for their only son. We all went to a hotel, where we met the Matchmaker, the girl's Parents and the girl herself. We drank orange juice and made conversation. I asked Dr Mossanen what the men were talking about, and he said they were comparing the Undergrounds in London, Paris and Moscow!

I was asked to make a few remarks in English to the girl as she was supposed to be fluent, but did not get much of a reply. Eventually the party broke up.

Outside I asked if the young man had found his prospective bride suitable.

'No,' said Madame Mossanen. 'The Mother squints and I would not wish to have grandchildren with bad eyesight.'

I asked the girls their view.

'Certainly not,' they said. 'Too short, we don't want short people in our family.'

'Something wrong with her teeth. Will NOT do,' said Soussan.

I then enquired what the young man had thought of his prospective bride.

'Most unsuitable,' he replied. 'I want someone more sophisticated. English or American perhaps.'

'You are not having THAT,' said his Mother sharply.

Next day I was woken by Madame telephoning. I could hear an angry voice at the other end so I asked her what was happening.

'It is the Matchmaker,' she answered. 'We have told him the girl is not suitable, and of course he was promised two of the best carpets if it went through. He is now protesting.'

There were, of course, difficulties of communication among us all. Dr and Madame Mossanen spoke no English and I spoke to them always in French; the children spoke English but no French; and I, of course, did not speak Farsi.

Dr Mossanen asked me if I would like to go for a trip with his wife and Soussan. It could be either the oil wells in the south or the Caspian, so I chose the latter, and we flew over the mountains to the Caspian Area, which was dominated by a huge Night Club building. We went down to the edge of the sea, and much to Madame's astonishment, I took off my shoes and stockings and went for a paddle. I had so often drawn the Caspian Sea on maps, and I was delighted to put my feet in it, and have my photo taken doing it.

We went up to the Russian border, and on the way back we had a puncture which delighted the inhabitants who came to watch. While the women in the rest of Iran were all heavily veiled in their *chuddars*, these women wore beautiful coloured dresses, but they objected to being photographed.

On our return there was great excitement as a matchmaker had rung to say he had found a very eligible young man for the elder daughter. This matchmaking took place at home, and a very grand salon which I did not even know existed, was opened up, dusted, and prepared.

Then the family differences broke out over what the elder daughter should wear. She was all for western dress, but the Matchmaker was summoned, and tried several dresses and alternate methods of make-up. Then a grand meal, at which were guests, was served. This Matchmaker was a woman, the other had been a man.

Next day everyone was in a state of preparation. The new dress and make-up were rejected, and Sohela insisted on wearing her white trouser suit in defiance of her mother and The Matchmaker.

The young man, who was very shy arrived with his Mother and we spent the evening in desultory conversation. The next morning the young man rang up to say he wanted to come again, which was a hopeful sign and everyone was very excited. Apparently he must come twice more before he and Sohela are allowed to go out together. Then his family investigated to see if there is any hereditary disease, or mental instability.

Later Sohela told me the young man was not the right social class and they thought he was after her money. She said it was a pity he had a Mercedes and not a Chevrolet but I told her if she loved him, nothing else mattered. I do not think 'love' came into the affair at all, but I heard later the match never materialised.

I do not think I ever ate so much as I did in Iran. Every night we went out to some restaurant where it was impolite not to eat. We were always accompanied by all the relatives, and at the weekends we went out to lunch too.

But all good things come to an end and I was taken out and bought lavish and beautiful presents. I was very sad to leave the Mossanens, especially as I never knew what happened to them. When the revolution took place and the Shah was deposed, Dr Mossanen must have been in great danger. By this time Soussan had left St Felix and was back in Tehran, and Dr Mossanen cabled me to ask if I could book her in at some institution so that he could get her out. I managed to get Lucie Clayton to say she would have her, but I heard no more. I imagine they all went to the States as I know Dr Mossanen had money there, and I always hoped after all their kindness to me I should one day see them again.

On the last day I was having a final tour of the city with the elder daughter. 'You know,' she said, 'we were dreading having you to stay.'

'Why, because I would not understand your way of life?' I asked.

'Well, you see, Jewish people are very close-knit families and visitors can bring bad luck. Some visitors are like Leah, the sad eyed, others like Rachel, the bringer of good luck and happiness.'

'Oh dear,' I said, 'I hope I have not been a Leah.'

'Oh, no,' she said, 'two matchmakings in one week, a Rachel indeed.'

What a perfect ending to a wonderful visit!

Chapter 34

Visit of the Queen Mother

Every school likes to celebrate its anniversary, and in 1972 St Felix decided to impress everyone with its 75 years of life. As was usual, requests went out to the Royal Family to come and help celebrate. When the girls were asked which member of the Royal Family they would like to come they voted for the Queen Mother and the request was granted.

It was decided to mark the occasion by opening the newly enlarged and improved swimming pool. It was now the proper competition length, and a separate diving pool had been added. A swimming display was to be the highlight of the proceedings.

Preparations for the visit began weeks before. First the ADC came down to go through all the arrangements.

'Will the Queen Mother have a glass of sherry before lunch?' I inquired.

'No, she likes gin and campari, please,' he replied.

Then the royal helicopter came on a trial run. I invited the two RAF men in to have some coffee but they refused. 'We are not allowed to leave the helicopter,' they explained.

The gardener was working nearby so I suggested he minded the helicopter while they came in and they agreed, but when he returned there was a man inside the helicopter.

'What on earth are you doing there?' I asked.

'I live just down the road,' he replied, 'and I wanted to see the inside of a royal helicopter.'

'Get out at once,' I said, 'you might be putting a bomb in it.'

'I'm not,' he replied, and climbed out.

Then there were the invitation lists. Parents, Old Girls and Southwold residents, of course, but who else? The police insisted everyone invited must be known to me, but people rang up all the time asking for invitations. Then there was the problem of who should be presented. The other Heads of local schools, the Staff, the Very Old Felicians, but again many people were offended including Staff wives and husbands.

I was also worried about the lavatory at my house. It was always going wrong, and I seized the opportunity to get the Bursar to order a new one. Unfortunately though it arrived and was installed it had no seat, and seats apparently came from Liverpool. The whole week before the visit there was frantic telephoning; then it got lost en route and was finally discovered in a BR office in Birmingham; and it only turned up the day before the visit.

Early in the week before the visit, the Duke of Windsor died, and we feared the whole visit might be off. Calls went through to Buckingham Palace, and to our relief we heard it was on. As a result the Queen Mother came in mourning. She wore the Star of India, a beautiful diamond star, on her coat.

The School, of course, had to be super cleaned. Flowers were put everywhere, all the school uniforms went to the cleaner and the window cleaners worked overtime. The local taxi was told he had to be at hand in case the Queen Mother had to be rushed to hospital, but he refused at the last minute in case his elderly car got a puncture, so one of the Governors lent his Rolls. The school doctor was told to be present, and to be always within fifty yards of the Queen Mother, and the local hospital was alerted to have a bed ready in case she was ill. Finally all arrangements had to be made with the police, the Lord-Lieutenant, and the press. At the last minute a call came from the Suffolk County Council to say they had not been invited, and they had to come too.

However, at last the great day came and the red royal helicopter hovered over the playing fields. This was the only occasion when the weather let St Felix down as a terrific storm broke out just as the helicopter landed. Fortunately the Lord-Lieutenant, Lord Stradbroke had a huge umbrella, and he guided the Queen Mother into my house. Most of the reception committee were soaked!

The lunch had been prepared with great care, and we had borrowed the head waiter from the Swan Hotel as I did not feel our maids could cope. Unfortunately he felt faint in the middle of lunch, and retired to the kitchen where he fainted, and was revived by the detective who was having his lunch with the housekeeper! So the two maids had to carry on to their great delight.

After lunch the Queen Mother had a short rest and then as the sun had come out, we started out for the swimming pool. The Chairman, Dr Chesney, the only woman in England with a double doctorate, accompanied us. She had travelled down in her doctor's robes, and was a little surprised, on meeting one of the Governors, to be told, 'Oh, Dr Chesney, what a nice mackintosh you have on.'

The domestic Staff were assembled outside my house, and they were the only ones who got good photos. The Queen Mother stopped and spoke to them which gave them great delight. Then on to the playing field where everyone was assembled. Parents, Old Girls, Staff, heads of local schools, Scouts, Guides, Cubs and Brownies, and Southwold people. All the people to be presented were supposed to be in the front row of chairs, but some had changed places to be with their friends, which rather put me out, as it was difficult to remember the newcomers' names, and several worthies got left out.

We proceeded to the swimming pool, planting a tree on the way. This was supervised by old Moore, one of the gardeners, who had been battling with me all the week because he had never worn a tie, and was not going to do so even on this occasion. It was only when I bought a black one, and told him it was for the Duke of Windsor that he agreed. While the Queen Mother was planting the tree, I looked up and saw a group of local boys from Lowestoft watching. How they had got in I could not think as they had been banned from the school some time before when they were annoying the girls of Gardiner House on Sunday afternoons. May is not a very good time for planting trees, and

Visit of the Queen Mother to St Felix 1972

unfortunately the tree died, and I had to plant another at dead of night. It amused me later on when visiting the school to be taken down to see it!

And so to the swimming pool where, fortunately, a covered-in dais had been erected, and with ever gathering clouds I was glad to see it. The Queen Mother graciously declared the pool open, and the display began. The rest of the school were assembled round the pool, and at that moment the heavens opened again, and they all got soaked.

'Are you going to allow all those girls to get wet?' asked the Queen Mother.

'Yes Ma'am,' I replied, knowing if they lost their places, I should never get them assembled again.

'You are a hard woman!' she responded, laughing.

Fortunately the rain stopped and everyone could enjoy the display given by the less academic girls who seldom were allowed to be in the limelight. Meanwhile my sister, Rosemary was taken to be the Bishop's wife, and was much flattered, and someone's best hat blew off into the pool and someone had to dive in after it.

The next event was touring the class rooms, and the partially sodden girls had to rush back to their class rooms, find their Form Staff and smile sweetly. The Queen Mother went through talking to everyone, and even addressing the French mistress in French! By then I had changed into academic dress, which seemed more fitting when touring the school.

At the end of the tour the architect was presented, and then we went back to my house for tea.

Here the Sixth Form were assembled. There had been great excitement over new dresses, what they should say, and who would hand round what. A Nigerian girl among them was particularly thrilled, and talked about her country and its people. Some were sitting at the Queen Mother's feet, and altogether it was a delightful party, graced by my Mother's best Coalport tea set.

All too soon the visit came to an end. The sun had now come out and everyone gathered on the playing field where the helicopter was waiting. There were many farewells, and soon the Queen Mother had said goodbye to everyone, and climbed into the helicopter. I thought she was very brave to travel about in it when it was so noisy, but she did not seem to mind.

At last it lifted off the ground, blowing all our hats away and raising a cheer from everyone assembled below. The last we saw of the Queen Mother was a little white gloved hand waving to us.

Then all the guests had to have tea, and those who had not seen the school went round. Most of the girls dived into the swimming pool, or amused themselves by giving interviews to the Press. The police departed, and the reporters followed. The unused Rolls Royce which had stood by all day went home. The school doctor, glad her services had not been required also left.

To end a lovely day, my brother Rowland had a dinner party for those of the family who had been there, and we were able to discuss the whole visit. Everything considered and in spite of the un-St Felix-like weather the visit had been a great success, and we were all full of admiration for a very gracious lady.

Finally the celebrations for the seventy-fifth anniversary ended with a church service in beautiful Southwold Church, taken by the Bishop of Norwich.

Chapter 35

Sabbatical

In 1973 I would have spent fifteen years at St Felix, just as I had done at Craighead, and now I felt it was time to go and find something else to do. But there were difficulties. One was that the Chairman, Dr Chesney was retiring and it was not a good idea for Headmistress and Chairman to go together; then I had lost five years of superannuation from teaching overseas, and my pension looked like being somewhat meagre unless I did a further five years; and my house in Eynsham was occupied by an American, who was acting as Vicar of the village during an interregnum, and it would be difficult to turn him out.

On the other hand, I had been offered a job in Nigeria, and had a number of other overseas posts in mind. The Governors pressed me hard to stay, pointing out I was quite fit, and the school going well, so in the end I agreed to stay the extra five years provided I could have a sabbatical term, before the five years began. Looking back I can see it was the wrong decision because the new Chairman had different ideas from me on how the school should be run, and those last five years were very unhappy.

However, at the end of 1972 I set off on my sabbatical. For many years I had longed to go to South America and now some St Felix Parents, Phil and Jill Appleyard invited me to spend Christmas with them in Lima, Peru. I then saw in *The Times* a coach trip advertised for £600, going from Lima to Rio de Janeiro, and I persuaded my cousin Katherine to go on it with me. Unfortunately just before we left, she had the bad news of her sister-in-law's death and as she was the executor, she had to cancel at the last minute, which was very sad.

I had a grim journey to Lima, as there was dense fog over Europe, and we had to divert from Holland to Genoa and then to Lisbon, so we arrived very late, though it was lovely flying in over the Andes.

Phil and Jill gave me a wonderful holiday in Lima which I shall never forget. Phil was doing a project on fishing for the United Nations and they had a beautiful house with a swimming pool. They showed me all the wonderful things in Lima, the Japanese Museum, the marvellous Gold

Museum, with the Inca treasures, the Cathedral where Pizarro was buried, and the lovely Spanish houses with their balconies. Most rich Peruvians spent their winters abroad so that they had a perpetual summer.

The Barriendas were the great contrast. In them lived the very poor, and it is difficult to imagine such poverty in any other country. People lived huddled under a sheet of cardboard, and spent their time searching the dustbins of the rich. All this in contrast to the well organised empire of the Incas, where no one starved, and fish was carried up from Lima to Cuzco daily. It was in contrast, too, to the splendid churches full of gold and silver, with the priests robed in cloth of gold, studded with jewels.

Phil Appleyard was trying to improve things by concentrating on the fishing industry, setting up refrigerators, teaching people how to gut and clean fish, and importing fish and chip vendors from Britain.

By this time I was getting very anxious about the trip round South America as, since Katherine was not coming, I had to go alone. The kind Appleyards took me to the bus, and I found myself the only English person among a group of Australians on their way home. There were forty-eight in our bus (there were two) and someone called out, 'There's a nasty Pommy in our bus.'

'Yes, there is,' I retorted, 'and just you be nice to her.'

Soon after we had started Uncle Tom (as our guide was nicknamed) came round and said, 'The best way to arrange the sleeping, is for everyone to sleep with the person who is beside them on the bus.'

'Are you game?' asked the Australian dentist who was sitting next to me. His one aim was to jump out at every stop to have a beer.

I replied in the negative, and found myself sleeping with a French lady doctor who bullied me unmercifully, until she got fed up and decided to have a single room, leaving me to pay for the double room. Later I slept with a Swiss girl, who slept in the nude, and then with two Australian girls, who lived in a mass of untidiness.

Our first stop was at Nasca, one of the most curious places in the world. It is covered with lines, and no one knows how they came there. Some say the Incas came from outer space, and these were guide lines to bring them to the heart of the world, but they are clearly visible not only from the air but from the ground.

From there we toiled up a terrifying road towards the Andes. At intervals there were little home-made crosses and bunches of flowers, marking the spots where previous coaches had gone over the edge. We ascended from sea level to 17,000 feet and everyone began to feel rather queer before we reached the ancient city of Cuzco. This was a place I had always wanted to visit and it was quite up to expectations. Cuzco was, of course, the ancient capital of the Incas, and we saw their fabulous stone walls made without mortar, and their great Parade Ground. In contrast there were the signs of Spanish occupation with the great Cathedral of St Francis. We were taken out to a market at Pisac which was very colourful and I bought a pullover covered in Inca signs.

By this time I was beginning to feel very queer. This was probably due to the great height, or maybe the food which was often served on dirty plates – and the kitchens were indescribable. I was sick all the time and lived on anti-sickness pills and bottles of Fanta.

Next day was the highlight of the tour – the visit to the lost city of the Incas, Machu Picchu. We set off early to catch the train, but I felt so ill I could hardly walk, and when we got to the station, I fainted on the platform. A kindly porter picked me up and said, 'Missy no go?'

'Missy go,' I said firmly, and added, 'Help me into the train,' which he did.

My face was streaming with blood but I mopped it up, and as it was a fairly long journey had time to recover. I was able to buy two more bottles of Fanta on the way, which helped. It would have been sad indeed to come all that way, and miss the highlight of the tour.

No one quite knows which Incas lived in this great hillside city. Some think it was for women only, and the men just visited it on state occasions. It was discovered by an American in 1913 and contains the remains of a royal palace, food storage places, houses, temples and meeting houses all in a good state of repair on the terraced slopes. It was altogether a wonderful day.

Next day we left Peru and I could not help being somewhat sad when I thought of the marvellous Inca civilisations destroyed by the Spaniards, and the poverty and wretchedness we had seen.

At the frontier to Bolivia there was an extraordinary scene as everyone seemed to be engaged in smuggling. We went on across the Altiplana full of little Indian dwellings, llamas, vicunas and alpacas. Suddenly we saw La Paz away down the valley and went down a winding road to it. It was just like any modern city, but we soon saw the beggars and little children holding out their hands for money. However, it had some splendid buildings and we had the best meal of the tour in the evening.

Next day we went to Lake Titicaca, a huge lake full of reeds. We went in a reed boat and landed on one of the reed islands. We had been asked to take pencils for the children but I thought there might be a surfeit and took balloons instead. On landing we were welcomed by the Seventh Day

Adventist priest who was in charge of the island, and were soon surrounded by hordes of children. I held out my balloons and they snatched them and ate them! They were quite the dirtiest children I had ever seen and their hair was covered in lice.

We left Bolivia and on to Chile, which was then ruled by Allende. We went through terrible deserts, and when we stopped for something to eat, the people said they had nothing for themselves. After a long journey we got to Antofagasta.

One of the problems I had to face each night was finding someone with whom I could go in search of a place to eat. There were no lights in any of the small towns and the only way to find a restaurant was to go round sniffing. On this occasion we had just started out when we became aware a man was following us and when we got to the restaurant he came across and said, 'I need dollars. Have you any?'

'No, we have none at all,' we lied, and he went back to his meal.

When we left he was waiting beside the road and said, 'I'm in trouble. I must go over the mountains tonight. Give me some dollars, and I will give you five times the value for each one.'

So we handed some over, and hurried back to the hotel, where we found the police had arrested two Frenchmen for changing foreign currency, which was against the law. We vanished to our rooms happy we had enough money to cover our entire stay in Chile.

Next day more deserts on the way to Santiago, where again we found a modern city with a great statue of the Virgin, given by the French, dominating it. We went out to the Port of Vina del Mar and had a very cold swim.

There remained the problem of how to get rid of our Chilean currency as we were not allowed to take it out of the country. In the end we decided to give a party in the hotel and invited all the Chilean guests. However at the end, we found they had paid for it, and had to go dancing down the main street of Santiago, throwing money to the beggars sleeping in the doorways.

Next day we went through a series of tunnels and passes into Argentina, where we saw the pampas, peopled by gauchos and innumerable cattle. Here there was plenty of food and everyone was smiling. Buenos Aires was a light, happy city and we enjoyed the night clubs where they did their famous Bottle Dancing, balancing six or seven bottles on their heads. I had several introductions here and was taken round everywhere. Most of the Australians flew home as they had had enough, leaving only eighteen of us from the original forty-eight to go on.

Beginning to feel rather tired and jaded we went on to Uruguay and Paraguay where the redoubtable Dr Stroessner was Dictator. So on to a wonderful day at the Iguassu Falls, which are one of the great sights of the world.

From there we drove on through the Mato Grosso in Brazil visiting the snake park in Sao Paulo, where more VWs are made than in Germany. So at last we came to Rio de Janeiro and saw the great figure of Christ towering above the city. We went to Petropolis to see the Royal Palace, and enjoyed seeing the huge football stadium and the Copacobana beaches.

With what money I had left I went up to Brasilia which is a marvellous modern city. Most of it including the breaktakingly lovely Cathedral was designed by Niemayer, and I was most impressed by everything. The Brazilians, however, do not like living there and get away when they can.

On the way back I had my final adventure. The plane refused to start and we had to go in a larger one which went to the International Airport, outside the city. It was midnight and I had no idea how to get back to my hotel so I asked two black ladies if I could share their taxi. They agreed but dropped me in the negro quarter and the taxi refused to go further. After battling through groups of fighting drunks I did find another taxi and got safely back.

So to catch the plane and get back to St Felix who were waiting with lighted torches to light me back after a very adventurous and happy sabbatical.

Chapter 36

Last Years

The last five years passed peacefully at St Felix. While other independent schools were having hard times, and in spite of its isolation, St Felix prospered.

Soon after I got back from South America I said to the secretary on the first day of term, 'What a nice peaceful beginning to term. I don't think we have ever had such a peaceful beginning.'

Ten minutes later cars started arriving full of Parents and girls who had arrived at Hawnes School, near Bedford, only to find it closed. There were pathetic tales of what had happened. One new girl had arrived from Brazil only to find the door shut; two Parents had saved up for years to send their daughter to this school in her new and expensive uniform only to find the school shut; and bewildered older girls looked with distaste on a school so different from the one they had left.

We took those we could by putting in extra beds, but it was not very many and the rest went off searching for other schools in the neighbourhood. We had a special responsibility as Hawnes had been founded by ex-St Felix Staff, and the previous Head was living in Southwold.

By 1978, when I retired the school was completely different from the one to which I had come in 1958. The numbers had grown from just over 200 to over 400 and we had even tried the experiment of having day boys in the Sixth Form. Day girls had been re-admitted and formed a substantial part of the school and there was now more visiting and three weekends when girls could go home. Most Parents were finding staying at local hotels too expensive, especially when it meant entertaining their daughters' friends as well. Some bought holiday cottages in the neighbourhood, others bought caravans and parked on the playing fields.

This meant we saw more of Parents, and were able to have Parents Meetings for all groups. Certainly girls were no longer just sent off to a school which the Parents had heard about. Instead there were endless tours of the school taking Parents with notebooks in hand, checking on all the facilities.

The shy girls of 1958 had vanished. The Sixth Form no longer wore uniform and were mature and well poised. Most of the senior school had some sort of boyfriend, and dances with boys' schools took place every term. There were many school visits too, not only geography courses, but skiing trips, and language courses in France, improved out of all recognition with the building of the language lab, and the interchange with French schools.

Each summer term we welcomed French and Swedish girls whose continental term had finished, and wanted to spend three or four weeks in an English school. Most of them found an English boarding school rather amusing.

We always had a fear of fire at St Felix, and on one occasion the Fire Brigade were invited to demonstrate that the girls could be rescued from the top dormer windows in the houses. I was watching the exercise as each girl, clad in striped pyjamas came down in a fireman's arms. Suddenly there appeared over the fireman's shoulder a vision in a very scanty silk nightie, shrieking in French. I would have loved to read her letter home after that episode!

Being an isolated school meant we had our share of Peeping Toms, and inquisitive schoolboys from Southwold. One night I was woken by the police who had been summoned to Nightingale House where the Sixth Form lived. Boys had been reported looking in at the windows.

'We can't find the night watchman,' remarked a burly policeman.

'I'll come down,' I replied, and putting on my dressing gown went to wake the caretaker.

'Better shut your door, Miss,' the sergeant suggested, and I did.

By the time we got down to Nightingale House, the boys had gone, and the caretaker had turned up. We said goodnight to the Police and went to look for the missing night watchman, who was supposed to be on his rounds.

The caretaker went to look for him in the school while I waited in his office. He came back smiling.

'I've found him, Miss,' he said, 'asleep on the sofa in your study.'

So it was goodnight to the caretaker and a message for the night watchman to see the Bursar in the morning. When I got back to my house, I found the latch had gone down when I shut the door. At that time I had no housekeeper so the house was empty and on my instructions all ladders were kept locked up in case anyone tried to climb in at night. I tried phoning the houses who were all asleep and finally got a bed in the

San, returning to my house in Sister's car, while the girls were having breakfast.

Punishments, too, had changed. Lines and learning poetry had long since gone and gating was used only in extreme circumstances. The worst punishment was extra prep on Thursday night which meant missing *Top of the Pops*.

By 1978 there were telephones in all the houses and there was frequent chatting with Parents. All Sixth Formers had study bedrooms, and all housemistresses and matrons had flats of their own.

Yet for me personally these last years were the most difficult of all. I hurt my back digging the herbaceous border in my garden, and for nearly a year was in great agony. The Head Girl had to haul me upstairs to take Assembly and I often wondered if I would be able to get to school in the morning. I had to go everywhere by car. No doctor seemed able to help, except to suggest I went off school, and it was not until the summer holidays of 1977 that I went to the Nuffield Orthopaedic Hospital in Oxford, and the world famous, Professor Duthie put it right.

This was followed by a case with one of the Housemistresses under the Industrial Relations Act. The governors had agreed that a Housemistress

Farewell to St Felix April 1978

209

who refused to have fire practices, and let the girls wander about by themselves in an area where there were several mental hospitals would have her contract terminated. We had a long and protracted case in Bury St Edmunds, when the tribunal were very hostile to independent schools, and the special lawyer from London was more worried about the imminent arrival of his first child than the case. So we lost it, and fortunately did not have to keep her. Later on I found she had taken another school to another tribunal.

Finally an event happened which I had always dreaded, when one of the Sixth Form was killed outside the school. She was wearing a black coat, was late back and walking along a road with no footpath. Another St Felix girl who had just left was going in her Mini to feed her horses, and not seeing her, killed her. It was one of the most terrible moments in my life, telling the Father, speaking to the girls in Chapel, and wondering if it could have been avoided. It had been the night of the staff play, and we were having a party afterwards, when the School Doctor came to tell us.

So I came to the end of my time at St Felix. There were the weeks of showing possible successors round the school, chosen from over 160 applicants, many of them men. Finally Mrs Anne Mustoe was chosen, and everyone was pleased. She was young and energetic and full of new ideas.

Then came the endless farewells. Many people do not realise that to a Headmistress pupils are like children and there is often great affection between them. It was perhaps less at St Felix than at Craighead because at St Felix the girls' first loyalty was to their Housemistress, but nevertheless it was a great wrench to say goodbye to both girls and Staff.

Later I was to be accused of staying too long at St Felix. It was perhaps a mistake as the new Chairman wanted to make a change and have someone younger, and I think no one realises that the bond between Heads and Schools is hard to break.

The leaving presents came. One suggestion was a hi-fi set, but not being musical I chose a beautiful Spode dinner set (from the Parents): a tea set from the Old Felicians; and a coffee set (from the Governors).

All the last year I was preparing for my successor, Mrs Mustoe, writing testimonials for the Staff; up-to-date records for Parents and girls; and careful notes on the way the school had been run.

Finally the last farewells, parties for school and Staff; many gatherings with friends in Southwold; and finally the official farewell from Governors and Lord Stradbroke.

Next day the girls left and I waved goodbye for the last time and went back to pack the last of my belongings. Never again would I live in such a lovely house or in such comfort. I was packed up and on a cold April morning, I set off down the St Felix drive waving goodbye to the faithful Peggy who had been my able domestic Staff over the last five years.

RETIREMENT

Chapter 37

Retirement

Many people dread retirement. I had looked forward to it.

A Headmistress in a boarding school has to forego many pleasures and I had often looked at the pages in *The Times* with concerts, plays and films which I would have loved to have seen, but could not get away. Even the school holidays were full of school business like scanning O and A level results, or the endless hunt for Matrons and Housemistresses. Even in the interval between my Mother's death and the funeral I had to go up to London to interview a member of Staff, who could not come any other time.

The first problem was where to live. Obviously I must get away from Southwold and not embarrass my successor. A big town was too impersonal, and in the end I decided to go back to Eynsham where I had lived as a child and still knew a few people. While I was thinking about it I was talking to an old parlourmaid who still lived in the village and she said, 'Oh, Miss Mary, you wouldn't leave us, would you?'

I still had my Mother's house, which I had bought from my brother, and upon leaving Southwold, I made my way there. It had been let for ten years and was in an indescribable mess, so I was fully occupied for the next few months.

The second problem was that I did not think I could live alone after thirty-five years of living among people. The thought of being by myself all the time did not appeal to me.

However, this problem was temporarily settled by finding a New Zealand friend, Marion Cocks Johnstone who was retiring after many years teaching gardening there. She was English by birth and had trained as a gardener at Studley, and after some time in New Zealand and South Africa had gone to live in New Zealand. We decided she would do the garden and I would do the house.

Unfortunately this did not work out. At first Marion or CJ as we liked to call her found it difficult to adjust to the English way of life, and after a year went back to New Zealand. However, on second thoughts that did

215

not work out either, and she decided to return bringing all her possessions with her. By this time she was getting very infirm, and increasingly deaf. Then she found difficulty in walking and I was having to dress and bath her, and take her out in a wheelchair. Eventually she herself decided to go into a home in Cheltenham where I visited her each week until she died some weeks later.

Left alone I found I could manage as by now I had many friends, but I found the house and garden too big so I sold up and moved to a house round the corner. It was just as well as shortly after I had left the chimney in the old house fell down through the roof and nearly killed everyone.

I was much happier in a small modern house which was often filled with visitors from overseas or young relatives wanting to talk about their futures. Very soon I was offered all sorts of jobs. The Vicar asked me to continue as a Lay Reader and I became a sort of unofficial curate! I was elected to the Parochial Church Council, Deanery and Diocesan Synods, education, schools and pastoral committees and served on the Thomas Commission for the reorganisation of the Diocese. I addressed the Diocesan Synod on unemployment and once took its opening prayers.

It was also nice to keep some contact with the schools and I was elected to the Governors of the Eynsham Primary School, the Bishop Kirk Middle School in Oxford, and St Mary's in Wantage. For a time I was a member of the GAP committee for finding occupation for students from all over the world for the time between school and university.

Perhaps the most interesting job was assisting with the Debenhams' Scholarships. Each year the store set aside £5,000 for scholarships for their Staff and their children. There were grants for elderly assistants who wished to take a needlework course; or music lessons for brilliant children to take a course of music lessons; and book tokens for hard pressed university students. We always had a splendid lunch in the Directors' Dining-Room, spent the afternoon going through the applications, and were then driven back to Paddington with a substantial cheque. Unfortunately the scheme came to an end when Debenhams was taken over by another firm.

Eynsham is a village with many thriving societies, of which there was a wide range, history, horticulture, art, choral to mention only a few. Yet all of them catered for the middle aged and the old. There were Scouts and Guides for the young teenagers but nothing for the other 14 to 16-year-olds. There was nothing for them to do but roam the streets at night, while the Church Hall stood shut and empty.

It was for them that I started a boys' club on Friday nights. We had coffee and sandwiches, pool and snooker, chess and darts, and round games for the younger ones. A small group brought their homework and did it in the kitchen. From the beginning it was clear that the church members were opposed to the idea because it was not open only to church members, and it was hard to get help. Sometimes I was left with only two helpers and thirty-two boys. As time went on the Parochial Church Council started trying to close the club on the grounds of lack of discipline or leaving the hall untidy but I battled on. Finally I got a formal complaint but on the night to which it referred the club was not open!

The boys were certainly a tough lot. When we had a Christmas party and played progressive games everyone cheated like mad. Finally I took action.

'You can't score at all at that table,' I told Wayne, one of the most unruly.

'You bloody old bitch, you can't do that to me,' he shouted.

'For that you can go home and not come back,' I ordered, and sent him home with a note to his Mother saying I would not have him in the club unless he apologised.

However, next week he was there again, and I was wondering what to do when he took the floor, and stamped on it.

'Shut up, you lot,' he called out, 'I'm sorry for what I said last week. It's just I have a bad temper and I did not mean it. This is a jolly good club, and we ought to be proud of it.'

Peace was restored and Wayne was forgiven.

I carried on with the club for nearly ten years, but when a Curate was appointed I was glad to hand it over. It was a disappointment to the boys and to me, when it became a small group of religious boys from good homes and most of them were excluded. It was to be on Sunday nights only but fortunately a new Youth Club was founded in the village, so they were able to go there as it had its own premises.

Still I was able to carry on with my Lay Reading, and used to have a packed church on the night of the fifth Sunday to sing Songs of Praise, and enjoyed going round some of the other churches in the district to preach or just to talk in the village hall. The vicar, Peter Ridley was a tower of strength, and he and I worked happily together until he went north to take a parish on the borders of England and Scotland.

Chapter 38

The Far East

Another charm of retirement is that you can take your holiday when you like, and are not tied to those times when everyone else is taking theirs. It was a great change not to be tied to April, August and September.

Before I left St Felix I had many invitations from the overseas girls who had come into the Sixth Form, and in 1983 I decided to accept some of the invitations from the Far East.

I flew from Bombay to Kuching in Sarawak. My passport had expired but I had a new one in my case. No one noticed at Heathrow, but there was trouble in Kuching until I had unpacked my case and taken it out. I had always wanted to go to Sarawak because as a child I had seen the White Rajah at a fete at Stanton Harcourt, and when Mr and Mrs Kulasingham, who had had a daughter at St Felix invited me to stay with them I was thrilled. They met me in Kuching when, because of delays en route, it was nearly midnight.

'Would you like to go to a hotel for the night?' they asked and added, 'or we could drive you home. It is forty miles and I am afraid it is a bandit infested road.'

I decided to risk it, and we reached Serian where they lived, quite safely.

Mr Kulasingham was working in a large secondary school. He and his wife were Indians and they lived in a delightful bungalow raised on stilts. There were only two bedrooms but their grown up son kindly moved in with them. It was incredibly hot and so was the curried food until Mrs Kulasingham made a special dish for me.

The first week was school holidays and the Kulasinghams were able to take me about. I saw the native bazaar, the pepper plantations, the marvellous Kuchchin Museum and the school itself.

The school was in the centre of a large area. The students often walked for two days with their packs on their backs to get there. They slept in long huts. Half the school had lessons in the morning; the other half in the afternoon. Those not having school were under the supervision of the teachers, and Mrs Kulasingham was very annoyed when one group were told to weed her garden and they dug up all the flowers. The discipline was good except at night when the students never seemed to sleep at all.

Sarawak had ceased to be ruled by the Brooke family after the war, and eventually became part of Malaysia. In its efforts to unite the country the Malaysian Government made Malay the official language, and the Indian and Chinese children had to do an extra year before starting school, so that they could learn the Malay language. English which had been the official language was dropped and gradually all the teachers were being supplanted by Malays.

While the Kulasinghams were teaching in the second week I had to amuse myself and I set off on an adventurous journey into the interior by bus. This was because I wanted to see the long houses. We had a very rough journey of one and three-quarter hours to Mongkos where there were two Chinese families running a store. They very kindly invited me to lunch, and then I persuaded one of the men to take me up to the long houses. He was taking stores in a rickety van. After thirty miles we reached the long houses and I was shown round. There were 150 families living in the first one. They were all Catholics, and had a crucifix hanging on the door of their area, and dried heads of Japanese soldiers, captured in the war, on the other side.

I had been asked to see a girl who had been at the school and was now working in the paddy fields. The head man organised everyone's work and they did what they were told.

I asked how she was getting on. 'Did you enjoy the school.'

'Yes, it was fabulous,' she answered and added, 'though what is the point of doing *Julius Caesar* for English O levels and returning to work in the paddy fields?'

I had no answer.

Another day I went again to see a school at Tabukau where two young VSO masters were working. However, they were having a holiday as the Indian headmaster, who was very good and popular, was being replaced by a Malay. The two VSOs were enjoying themselves and did not want to return to England!

All too soon my time at Sarawak came to an end, and to my dismay my next hostess who lived on a rubber plantation, and had a child at St Felix cabled to say she had had to go back to England and could not have me after all. However Mr Kulasingham kindly arranged for me to go to the YMCA in Singapore, and for a friend who was a judge to look after me. I was met by this Mr Lee, who was most kind and took me to see the

Chinese Bird Gardens, the Tiger Balm Monstrosity, the university and to Mount Faber to see the lights. He could not have been kinder and I was most grateful.

After a few days I went on to Penang by night to stay with some of the Kulasinghams' relations. It was a most perilous journey across the Causeway, and we had to change buses at the other end. Meanwhile I had an extraordinary meal in a cafe with some Indians and then could not find the next bus. In the end I did find it and, dragging my suitcase, got gratefully into it, arriving in Penang in the early morning.

The Kanandas were most generous and kind. They had a beautiful house and, being Hindus, took me to several of their temples and drove me round the island. I went to the Penang Club with its memories of British rule and pictures of all the British officials who had ruled in Penang.

But the event I shall always remember is sitting by the sea in the evening with Mrs Kanandas when she told me how she was married at fourteen to a man she did not know but it had turned out happily. She was worried about her daughter Eswary who at nineteen was still unmarried. Eswary was very musical and often played the piano to us in the evenings.

By now I had a letter from another St Felix parent, Mrs Sim so I was able to go on to stay with the Sims in Kuala Lumpur. The Sims were Chinese and Buddhist. They had the most beautiful house with many servants, and I had a lovely room complete with bathroom. Again I was royally entertained, going to Chinese restaurants, Batik factories and to dinner with many friends. I was even taken to a Chinese beauty parlour at the Sims' expense, and thoroughly enjoyed it.

It was unfortunately with the Sims I had the most embarrassing episode in my life. They gave a very grand dinner for me in a Chinese restaurant. I put on my best frock which had a zip down the back, and in the middle of the meal the zip went. I summoned the waitress and asked her to get a safety pin and pin it up but she did not understand and Mrs Sim had to explain to her. I spent the rest of the meal in agony in case it split again. It does apparently happen to zips in hot weather!

The Sims had three girls and one son, the youngest girl still at home. The boy was at Felsted, and wanted to be a doctor. When Mrs Sim asked whether I had any relatives who were doctors, I had to confess I did. She implored me to help in the matter. However, when I got back to England, I found the son had already made all his plans and was quite satisfied that he would be accepted for military training.

The Sim family were preparing for Chinese New Year which meant a whole set of new clothes and we spent a long time in the warehouse choosing them. I was able to buy some lovely Batik materials, at the same time.

There were still a few days before my plane went. It had been rather an anxious holiday wondering where I would go next, and if I might have to go to a hotel which I could not afford. The Kulasinghams had suggested I visited their relations in Thailand, and I would have loved to have gone, but time was too short.

I was sorry to leave the Sims who had been so kind and generous. It is always fun to live a very luxurious life, surrounded by servants who cater for every whim. I enjoyed meeting all their friends and relations and living in their beautiful home.

Fortunately I remembered there was a St Felix Old Girl living in Kuala Lumpur, and since I had nowhere to go I rang her and asked her if she could put me up for two nights before I caught the plane. Jane Jones, as she had been at school, was now married with one small son, and said she would be delighted to have me, and I enjoyed the visit with them. Mrs Sim came over and took me to a Japanese lunch as she said it was the one thing she had forgotten to show me!

So ended a wonderful tour of the Far East. Though sometimes rather anxious about where I would stay next, I had been so well looked after and entertained that I shall never forget it.

Chapter 39

Summer School

I often thought that my main contribution to the scholastic world was as a teacher, rather than an administrator. So I regretted very much that my teaching days, as I thought, had come to an end. However, just before I retired I took a course in teaching English to foreigners, thinking I might do some coaching of overseas people. Then I saw an advertisement in the *Oxford Times* for a teacher in a summer school for foreign students, and of course, I could not resist the temptation.

The organiser was Robert, who curiously came from Southwold, and took me on condition I drove a minibus. I had never driven one before but hoped I could manage. I did not realise at the time it involved driving the students round London.

The students were mainly from the Universities on the Continent, and in the early days were divided into three classes, later on into six. The course was English Literature except for the bottom class who were mostly young boys whose parents had gone on holiday and wanted to get rid of them. Most of the time I taught them.

Besides teaching there were the expeditions, and I found myself with a busful going to London. I was supposed to point out the sights as well as drive, and this proved difficult.

When we crossed Waterloo Bridge the students called on me to stop. 'Please recite Wordsworth's poem, Miss.'

I did my best with traffic roaring around and people hooting madly at me. Then on to Baker St, and I pointed out where Sherlock Holmes had lived, narrowly missing two bicycles and a pedestrian. Oxford Street followed, and a demand to go down Wimpole St to look at the Barrett's house.

Perhaps the worst was going round Hyde Park Corner, I could not find the right lane and the students began to ask how many times we were going round.

'You just don't understand,' I explained, 'this is a most interesting part of London, and you will see the house where the Duke of Wellington

222

lived, the old St George's Hospital, and if you look very hard you might see Buckingham Palace.'

Perhaps the worst drive was when there was a rail strike and I had to drive the minibus down to Folkestone, to pick up the students. I got lost on the way back and thought I was the last as there were no other minibus drivers, but they had had breakdowns and were after me.

Finally, of course, I had a slight smash, scraping a lorry standing at the back of D H Evans, but fortunately there was only a long scratch, and Robert who was insured was very nice about it, especially as the Music Master taking the girls to a concert had driven into an underground car park whose roof was too low, and taken the top off the bus.

The teaching was a real joy, because most of the students knew about Shakespeare but had not read his plays and they loved them. We also had debates. One was on capital punishment, and the French girls complained that in France people could be guillotined for killing a policeman, but not for killing a policewoman.

In the same debate Boris, from Jugoslavia, asked what the position was there, said coldly, 'You must have capital punishment for enemies of the State.'

The highlights of the courses were the concerts and the gala evenings. Paul Roberts who was in charge of the music gave us some lovely concerts every year and many of the students were very gifted musicians. The concerts were enlivened by the Spanish girls who always liked to demonstrate a flamenco dance in the interval.

But it was the gala nights which were always the final excitement before the students went home. Every teacher had to put on a play and it fell to my lot to do a scene from Shakespeare. The first time I did the Witches Scene from *Macbeth* and realised too late I had taken on a formidable task. The three Spanish girls who were the witches found words like 'fenny snake' most difficult and we spent hours rehearsing. When we actually did it, a child screamed with fright and had to be taken out. The performance was in the Long Room at New College which was so narrow, it was very difficult to act in it.

But the most formidable was when Robert asked me to do the love scene from *Romeo and Juliet*, mainly because there was a little French girl who looked just like Juliet and a handsome Austrian who would make a perfect Romeo.

Unfortunately the little French girl knew very little English and the part was quite beyond her. Then one day a large French girl with a spotty face came to watch.

'She is no good,' She said (which was true). 'I was Juliet once in Paris and I should like to take the part.'

This upset Juliet so much that she refused to take the part at all and Romeo saw me privately and said if the large girl took the part, he would give up his part, too.

In desperation I went to all the classes appealing for a Juliet. This was Monday and the gala was on the Friday. Eventually I found a charming South African girl who said she would love the part, and I thought I was home and dry.

But no – there was the question of costume. What was Juliet to wear? In desperation I went round the village asking who had acting boxes, and brought several dresses for Juliet to see. She had learnt her part beautifully but refused to act without a dress she liked. So I went to the costume shop in the town but still no luck. I was desperate and warned Robert I might not be able to do the play.

Two nights before the gala I could not sleep and was reading a book when I looked down at my nightdress. It was a summer white one, very simple, and next morning I took it in. 'Just what I wanted,' said Juliet and harmony returned. The performance stole the show and *Romeo and Juliet* received great applause.

The students lived with families in Oxford. How Robert found them all I do not know, but some had to come in from as far as Kidlington.

One day one of the more timid girls asked to speak to me privately so I took her aside and asked what was upsetting her.

'It is my lodgings,' she said, bursting into tears. 'It's the Father, he makes advances to me.'

So I went to Robert and he found another family for her.

It was only later I realised there was another student in the same lodgings. 'Does the Father make advances to you too?' I asked. 'If you would like to move I am sure Robert would arrange it for you.'

'Oh no,' she replied, 'I like it.' There was no more to be said.

At first Robert was rather dubious when I suggested taking the students to Stratford to see a play but after the first year he agreed and with careful preparation it was a great success. Not entirely for me who had to drive them back in the dark along a road which was partly up. On arrival in Oxford they had to be delivered at their lodgings, and of course I did not know all the streets in the city. The students only knew their bus route, so I seldom got to bed on Stratford nights before 3am.

Towards the end of my time with the summer school, I became interested in the Pre-Raphaelites, and the students took this up with enthusiasm. Fortunately there was a big exhibition on at the Tate, and I was able to take the top class up in the minibus to spend the day there.

In the holidays Robert took plays all over the Continent, and booked new students at the same time. Eventually this took the place of the courses, though later he went back to them. By this time I had given up, but it was one of the things I enjoyed most in my retirement, and I look back on it with great thanks to Robert for giving me this opportunity.

Chapter 40

China

During my retirement up until 1993, I had many lovely holidays. A wonderful week in Rome and two holidays in the Algarve with St Felix parents; two further trips to New Zealand because it was so lovely to be with my Craighead Old Girls and other friends again; and a variety of package tours to Jugoslavia, northern Spain and Portugal, which included a visit to the great Cathedral of St James of Compostello; a week in Soviet Russia, and several trips with the National Trust, not only to Shrewsbury and North Wales, but also to Normandy and Alsace Lorraine. In 1992, I went for a holiday in Greece seeing all those places about which I had taught so often. The highlight of them all was a trip to China, which was one of the places I had always wanted to visit.

The local schoolmaster was a Chinese scholar and I discovered he took a trip every year, so with twelve others, including my cousin, I went with him. It was a long and exhausting flight to Beijing, and somewhat of a disappointment as we drove through darkened slummy streets. Because of a shortage of electric power, many of the houses had no light, and groups of people were playing scrabble or poker under the street lights. The hotel was very comfortable though it had obviously not been renovated since Victorian times.

However, next day we saw the real China, beginning with Tiananmen Square which was later to become so famous. It was full of grandparents airing small babies. The Chinese are only allowed two children at the most, and as both parents work it is the grannies who must mind the babies. None of them wore nappies, but just had a slit at the back!

From there we went to the fabulous Forbidden city where the Emperor lived with the eunuchs and the women. Hundreds of young men were rounded up to work there, and when the Emperor went out no one could look at him, and must draw their blinds.

We saw the incredible marble bridge brought down from the north on frozen streams; the ceremonial rooms; and the Emperor's throne with an opening behind from where the last Empress told him what to say.

From there we went on to the Temple of Heaven where the Emperor came every year to pray for a good harvest. Then on to the Summer Palace where the last Empress lived. She was the one behind the Boxer rebellion, and is said never to have cut her toe or finger nails!

Next day we went to the Great Wall. We were offered the easy or difficult way. I preferred the former but the rest of the party opted for the latter so I went too. As it was 94°F in the shade it was hard going but a kindly Chinese gentleman took my arm and helped me up to one of the towers. Coming down one of the party mistook the way and went down into Mongolia, which led to a panic but she was eventually brought back.

So to the Ming tombs via a long road carved with animals on both sides, and then we went up by minibus into Mongolia. The Chinese have tried to move people up there, and so they allow the people to have more children as an incentive. It is very hot in summer and snowbound in winter, so we saw the large mud stores for wheat and meat which they use when all else is frozen. We saw a Mongolian yurt or tent and actually slept in one which was most uncomfortable, and the sanitary arrangements were just a communal pit!

But the highlight of Mongolia was being allowed to ride on the steppes. First a sedentary walk on a camel and then full gallop on a pony. Everywhere there were miles and miles of open country, and it was a wonderful feeling. At night we had a display of Mongolian dancing and singing, and the following day saw a wonderful display of horsemanship.

Our next stop was Hoh Hot, one of the chief towns in Mongolia. It was here that some women in a clothing shop beckoned us to come in. They were making jeans but we could not make out what they wanted. Eventually it transpired they wanted to see what underwear European ladies wore. As it was very hot we had not much to show, but they had even less.

So to Datong where there is a fascinating collection of statues of Buddha, carved out of the cliff face. This was the only place where we got a somewhat hostile reception as they were obviously not used to foreigners.

From there we went to the great national shrine of the Jin Temple built some 1,200 years ago. The temple is built round an everlasting spring and the story goes that it was a very dry district and an old woman came to fetch water if she could. A whip appeared from heaven and she whipped what water there was and it has flowed ever since. We also saw the Hall of the Holy Mother, who was one of the last Empresses to live here. Usually the ladies-in-waiting were killed when she died so that she would have attendants in the next world, but she had statues made of them all and one of herself to do instead.

The next stop was Sian now famous for the Terra Cotta Warriors found by boys digging a well. This was the same idea, that instead of killing all the soldiers when the Emperor died they could be replaced by statues. Sian itself was once the capital of China, and its walls were being rebuilt. The soldiers were an incredible sight and one wonders how they ever restored both men and horses. I kept leaving and then returning to have a last look. Beyond, lies the mound with the Emperor's tomb, which some think when opened will rival Tutankhamun's.

Finally we came to Canton, a beautiful city on the Pearl River. Here we visited a commune where women were making fireworks. The people in the south were much more relaxed. After Beijing where everyone wore the same clothes and rode men's bicycles, we saw both men and women colourfully dressed and shops full of brightly coloured clothes.

This tour of China was not only seeing all the famous sites, but was called China Old and New, and we saw many interesting factories. On arrival the manager came and told us about his factory, then we went through it, and finally arrived at the shop where we bought its products.

We saw women making carpets, and doing incredibly small designs; lovely jade being made into miniature horses; and beautiful silks being imprinted. Most interesting of all was a railway complex. We stayed in the guest house where 8,000 workers and their families lived, and who had to ask permission to leave the area. It contained schools, hospitals, crèches and leisure facilities. We saw the engines being made and then we went on a ride on one. Because China has so much coal all the engines are powered by coal-fired steam.

The schools were on holiday but as all the Parents work they are kept open for leisure activities all the holidays. We toured one and watched while the kindergarten sang us songs, and the older children worked with computers or played in an orchestra.

We also visited a hospital. The Chinese have an alternative system of medicine with its own drugs, but we were rather horrified by what we saw. People were lying on wooden boards which looked most uncomfortable, and a nurse was going round giving injections using the same syringe for everyone! The whole place was old and falling to bits, but no doubt the hospitals in the big cities are quite different.

The people work six days and have one off, a different one in each factory, so there are never too many crowds, and we noted many people in little boats on the lakes, just sculling about happily.

No doubt the tourists only go to certain parts of the Republic, but we did not see any signs of repression, or police harassment. On the whole the people were smiling and pleasant. It was in Canton where we first saw an open market which was something new in China, and the people were arriving with ducks and vegetables which they could sell to make money for themselves instead of having to give it all to the State.

Finally we drove down to Hong Kong, passing the new Chinese Economic Zone, where the Chinese are preparing for the unification with Hong Kong in 1997. Over the border everything changed. People in bright clothes, cars everywhere, shops full of luxuries, and an atmosphere of gaiety and happiness. We went shopping and out to Aberdeen for a wonderful meal, and a farewell to Roger our guide who was leaving us to become headmaster of one of the schools in Hong Kong. We also had a woman guide the whole way, and in each town a local guide, with special knowledge, some very good, others having difficulty with their English.

So, loaded with presents, and feeling we now knew a lot more about China we caught the plane in Hong Kong, and set off home.

There was, however a strange sequel to the China trip. The night we spent in Sian, I started coughing, and continued all the way back to Britain. It did not stop there. It became impossible to go to lectures, to go out to dinner, or to attend a theatre. The local Doctor was puzzled; the Oxford specialist could find no cure; I spent a week in hospital, and drank every kind of Cough Mixture to no effect. This continued for nearly two years, and was finally diagnosed as a cough endemic in north east China, and the specialist wrote to the Medical School in Beijing. He go no reply, but at last one of the many antibiotics tried was effective and peace ensued!

Chapter 41

Last Days

One of the chief interests I had in retirement was my work as a Lay Reader. I was appointed as the second woman reader in the Anglican Church by the Archbishop of New Zealand; as the second woman Lay Reader in the English Anglican Church by the Bishop of Edmundsbury and Ipswich; and by the Bishop of Oxford as a Lay Reader in the Oxford Diocese.

I loved the work, preaching (with a Bishop's Licence), visiting country parishes, and taking a full part in St Leonard's Church, Eynsham in the time of two Vicars. The highlight was probably preaching in my own church on Armistice Day.

But all good things come to an end, and we had a new Vicar. When I asked him which services I should take, and when he would like to see me, he replied that he did not approve of women taking part in church services because it was contrary to the Bible. He suggested I attached myself to one of the other churches in the neighbourhood, but I did not want to go out by car all over the place, particularly on dark nights. So my Lay Reading was abruptly terminated, and for a long time after that I missed it terribly, especially when men with no qualifications preached, or took services.

However, I busied myself with other activities. It was interesting to join the University of the Third Age, and to join their History, Literature and Play Reading group, and for three years I was Chairman of the Eynsham Society which protected the interests of the village, arranged walks and looked after the footpaths and stiles. I was involved in a long struggle over the widening of the A40, when an inspector held an inquiry in Witney. In the end it was abandoned for lack of money.

We were also busy with a village Appraisal, giving a picture of the village and its activities.

Buy as I got older and could tell I was heading for hip trouble which would curb my activities, I knew I must go once more to New Zealand to say goodbye. I wanted my Craighead girls to remember me as I had once been, young and energetic, and to be spared the sight of me old and haggard! Accompanied by my cousin Everilde, I went twice to New Zealand, which was the end of a happy association.

We travelled via Fiji and Australia, where I went to stay again with Margaret who had been one of my PE mistresses in New Zealand. She was happily married and living in a lovely house on the North Shore. Her husband had a beautiful yacht, and we sailed round the coast, picnicking in one of the many bays. We also went to see The Rocks, which I thought was just a scramble but found it was where the convicts landed, and of course we went round the Opera House which was quite new then.

We flew on to New Zealand going to the North Island first on the first occasion and on to the South Island afterwards. It was Craighead's seventy-fifth anniversary, and Old Girls met us at every point.

When we got to Timaru there was a grand celebration day, with pictures of all the events of the past, and visits round any new additions. A picnic meal followed and then I was to speak. The noise as people ate their picnics, and reminisced about old times was terrific and the Chairman of the Old Girls came up to me and said, 'I don't think we can ever get them quiet, do you? Shall we abandon your speech?'

Having spent ages getting it ready I was certainly not going to do that, so I clapped my hands and said, 'Quiet, please, girls.' There was a dead silence, and I was able to begin.

Of course I wanted to visit the Chapel, and I found myself preaching again, and looking at the lovely oak pews, the beautiful east window, put in after I left, and the altar cloth worked by my Mother.

I was given a seat at the back, sitting next to one of the women governors, who said, 'What a lovely Chapel this is!'

I agreed!

Leaving Timaru we joined a coach trip, breaking the journey at Dunedin to see the Old Girls there, and on to Queenstown and Wanaka. The Americans were much amused at the coach continually stopping, as various Old Girls came down from the back country stations to see me even for a few minutes.

We were lucky on this trip as though we had booked second class there were no others on it so we were moved to the best hotels, ending up at the Hermitage, with happy memories of struggling over the Copeland.

So over the Lindis Pass, and back to Christchurch with memories of my dear Archbishop and his sister, and happy Christmases with all their family. Finally, escorted by a group of Craighead Old Girls, we made our way to Christchurch Airport and boarded the plane for Sydney. As we rose up off the airport, I looked back at the mountains, the great land seen first by Abel Tasman, 'The land uplifted high', and thought of all the happy days I had had there; of the women all over the country who had been in my care, and the walks and climbs I had done.

It was not quite the end of the New Zealand connection because in the summer months many Old Girls and their husbands came to call or stay, and twice I went to a party for the New Zealand schools at New Zealand House in London.

I also made a last trip to St Blaise in Switzerland, but unfortunately the school had come to and end. Some of the Staff were still living in the village, and greeted me with affection. I had happy memories of La Châtelainie too.

I could of course visit St Felix too, and I went down several times to visit the three Heads who succeeded me. There, too, we had Old Felician dinners, lovely concerts, and happy Parent Days, and I was so pleased to see some of my old Staff.

The years passed by, and I found myself celebrating my eightieth birthday in 1993. I had thought it would pass quietly but first there was a lovely lunch at St Hilda's for my godchildren. This was organised by my niece Lavender, and even the youngest, Tom Young, turned up with his mother.

My brother Rowland and his son and son-in-law had also arranged a party. This was held at the beautiful Shillingford Bridge Hotel on the Thames, and thirty guests were invited. They covered every aspect of my life. Yvonne my school friend, Richard my cousin whom I met at Malvern, Susan, one of my first pupils at Craighead, Mary Anne and Judy from the Châtelainie, and Daphne Gee from St Felix. There were various cousins who were delighted to see each other, and old friends I had not seen for years. Only my sister Rosemary was too infirm to come and my Oxford friend Vera was away on holiday.

So ended the long timetable, and I went into purdah to get my hips replaced!